Image Credit <a href="https://www.freepik.com/free-photos-vectors/business">Business vector created by macrovector - www.freepik.com</a>

About the Author

Jay Tarimala is an accomplished and internationally experienced (Canadian) recruitment and bid management professional with over fifteen years of hands-on experience in sourcing, recruiting, interviewing, candidate selection and proposal development.

Research Methods and Bid Management

Copyright © 2021 by Jay Tarimala

All rights reserved.

No portion of this document may be reproduced or shared or modified or transmitted in any form without prior permission from the author except in the cases of brief quotations for critical articles and reviews.

Author can be contacted thru email at indcaneto@outlook.com

DISCLAIMER AND TERMS OF USE

The buyer is granted a single, non-transferable license for his or her personal use of the book.

The contents of the book shall not be altered or reproduced or transmitted by the buyer in any way. The buyer is not authorized to create derivative works based on the contents of the book, nor use these contents in any way that would infringe the copyrights in this material.

The author or publisher is not providing legal or professional advice but, instead, is sharing ideas about research methods and bid management tactics that the reader may choose to consider. The Publication of this book does not create a consultant-client relationship.

This body of work contains links to third party websites and links that are not owned or controlled by the Author and the Author assumes no responsibility for the content, usage, privacy policies, or practices of any third party web sites or services.

The buyer further acknowledges and agrees that the Author shall not be responsible or liable, directly or indirectly, incidental or consequential for any damage or loss or injury or claim, caused or alleged to be caused by or in connection with use of or reliance on any such content referred to in the book or any such web sites or services.

This book is published for strictly educational purposes only. Hence, if you wish to apply the ideas or strategies referred to in this book, you are taking complete responsibility for your actions and the author and or publisher are not liable or responsible for any resulting damage or expense.

The author and or the publisher make no representations or warranties, express or implied, in fact or in law, with respect to the accuracy or completeness of the content of this book and specifically disclaim all warranties, including without limitation warranties of fitness for a particular purpose.

Every attempt has been made by the author to provide acknowledgment of the sources used for the material in this book. The author has put every effort to provide accurate information about research methods and bid management at the time of publication. Neither the author nor publisher assumes any responsibility for errors and omissions, or for changes that occur after publication.

Table of Contents

CHAPTER 1 BOOLEAN OPERATORS AND GOOGLE 9
- 1.1 Inurl operator 13
- 1.2 Intitle operator 14
- 1.3 Intext operator 15
- 1.4 Related operator 16
- 1.5 Filetype operator 17
- 1.6 Ext operator 19
- 1.7 AROUND (X) Operator 20
- 1.8 Number of words 21
- 1.9 Minus operator 21

CHAPTER 2 BING SEARCH ENGINE 22

CHAPTER 3 LINKEDIN 24
- 3.1 Linkedin X-ray 26
- 3.2 Country code filter 28
- 3.3 Linkedin country codes 28
- 3.4 Feed search 29
- 3.5 Certification search 30
- 3.6 Linkedin groups 32
- 3.7 Linkedin email address search 33
- 3.8 Personal branding 34

CHAPTER 4 SOURCING TOOLS 36
- 4.1 Free corporate email address search tool 37
- 4.2 Validating an email address 39
- 4.3 Prospect email engagement 40
- 4.4 Outreach management 40
- 4.5 Tool for Notes and timestamps for Google search 44

CHAPTER 5 TWITTER 45
- 5.1 Twitter X-ray 48

CHAPTER 6 FACEBOOK 51
- 6.1 Facebook X-ray search 51
- 6.2 Facebook native search 52

CHAPTER 7 COMPETITIVE INTELLIGENCE 54

- 7.1 X-raying a site 55
- 7.2 Techcrunch and Crunchbase 56
- 7.3 Newspaper and Financial magazine sites 56
- 7.4 Government planning departments 56
- 7.5 Patent, Technical db and Research publications search 57
  - 7.5.1 Google scholar 58
  - 7.5.2 Microsoft Academic 60
  - 7.5.3 Semantic Scholar 61
  - 7.5.4 Researchgate 62
- 7.6 Startups 63
- 7.7 Budget Knowledge 65
- 7.8 Alerts 66
- 7.9 Competitor websites 68
- 7.10 Competitor analysis tools 75
  - 7.10.1 SimilarWeb 75
  - 7.10.2 Mediatoolkit 78
  - 7.10.3 VisualPing 78
  - 7.10.4 Feedly 79
  - 7.10.5 Datanyze 79
  - 7.10.6 RivalIQ 80
  - 7.10.7 Craft 81
  - 7.10.8 Whatruns 82
  - 7.10.9 Builtwith 83
- 7.11 Trends 84
- 7.12 Research firms 85
- 7.13 Associations 86
- 7.14 Companies specializing in CI 87
- 7.15 Organization charts 88
  - 7.15.1 theOrg.com 88
  - 7.15.2 Scout by LeadIQ 90

CHAPTER 8 OTHER SEARCH AVENUES 92

- 8.1 Conference websites 92
- 8.2 File sharing sites 93
- 8.3 Image search 94

CHAPTER 9 FEDERAL BIDS 95

    9.1 US perspective 96

    9.2 Canadian perspective 103

    9.3 UK perspective 104

    9.4 Australian perspective 107

    9.5 EU perspective 109

CHAPTER 10 JOB DESCRIPTION 110

    10.1 How to write effective Job Description 112

CHAPTER 11 STAFFING YOUR TEAM 116

    11.1 Slideshare 116

    11.2 Emoji and symbol search 117

    11.3 APMP Awards 118

CHAPTER 12 BID MANAGEMENT DISCIPLINE 119

    12.1 Executive summary tips 119

    12.2 KPIs for a bid manager 121

    12.3 Account manager relationship with bid manager 122

    12.4 Proposalitis 123

    12.5 Incumbency – Advantage or a burden 125

    12.6 Are RFPs a noose or a necklace? 127

    12.7 Are the RFPs wired? 130

    12.8 Words and Phrases to avoid in business Proposals 133

    12.9 Word spellings to look for in business Proposals 139

    12.10 Persuasive writing 141

    12.11 Proposal Quality Validation 142

    12.12 Client Presentations 145

    12.13 Bid debriefing 147

    12.14 RFP Tricky clauses 149

    12.15 Win Loss Analysis 151

    12.16 Proposal Automation software requirements checklist 154

    12.17 Writing and Presentation tools 163

    12.18 Proposal Writer interview discussion points 166

    12.19 Bid Manager Interview discussion points 168

    12.20 Proposal writing books 171

Preface

Proposal writers and the larger bid management community have many concurrent proposals to work on and a part of the effort is oriented towards researching online to find latest trends, technology changes, competitor positioning, upcoming disruptive models etc.

They only need to get inspiration from the recruiters who look to find the needle in the haystack every day to find the right candidate to fulfill the hiring manager mandate. The search strings, productivity tricks and their ways of thinking they implement can be utilized by bid management teams to emulate them.

These are the times the upper management is asking for more productivity from the bid management community.

The days of proposal editing, compiling information from multiple sources and packaging the bid maybe coming to an end. The bid managers (no hands on or very little hands on skills) who are functioning as bid coordinators would be the ones who would feel the heat the most.

Employers may want to see more value added output like solution architecture, qualitative research, and more robust pricing estimates.

As margins come under pressure, the top management may introduce proposal automation software to improve productivity bottlenecks, so expect more workloads.

This exercise is an attempt to equip the bid management community with the various ways and methods to optimize their time and find the relevant information (budgets, trends, movers and shakers etc.) to be better prepared to deliver a more effective proposal.

Chapter 1 Boolean operators and Google

Without their knowledge, even a casual user would be using Boolean operators in search engines to find the necessary information. It's become such a commonplace now that it is hard to forecast a future without using them and recruiters by the nature of their craft swear by it.

There are close to 50 Boolean operators and Top Boolean 3 operators include "AND", OR, "-" (minus).

The AND, OR operators must be typed in uppercase letters to let Google know it is an operator and not a regular word.

AND operator takes precedence over "OR" operator and it limits your search.

OR operator expands your search results.

The order of priority for search is:

- Quotation marks (" ")
- Parentheses ( ) (nowadays Google seems to ignore parentheses)
- Minus
- AND
- OR

Tip 1: In Google, AND operator is automatically added to the string, so no need to type it explicitly.

Asterisk (*) helps in expanded search for a specific word.

Example develop* will return (develop OR developed OR developing OR development).

In Linkedin website, this Boolean modifier does not work but the usage of x-ray in Google, the '*' modifier works.

For a specific search as below, Google provides the number of results (1.43M).

Figure 1: Basic Google search

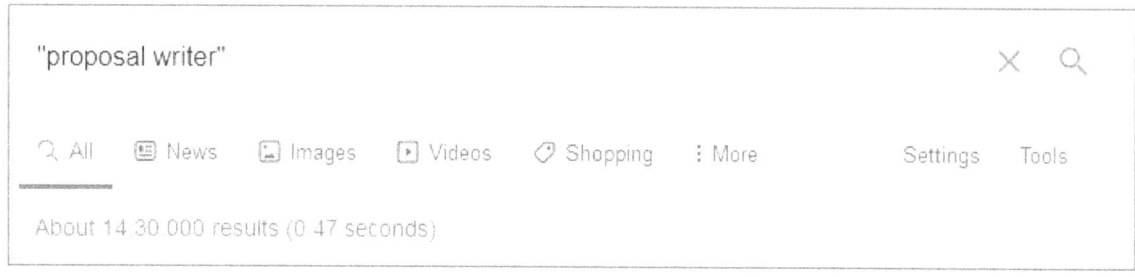

If you were to click the results page by page, it ends up like it is shown in the figure below

Figure 2: Basic Google search page navigation

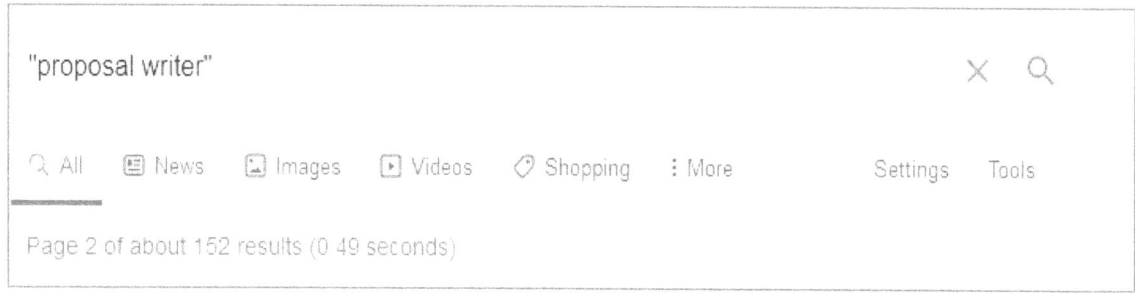

Notice the actual result is 152 instead of the 1.43M search links.

Tip 2: The maximum clickable links you may expect of such a search is 300 for the most part. However, if you used the "Images" tab, the same query may give much more results than 300 as it seems images has a separate database look up compared to a normal search.

Tip 3: You can reduce the number of clicking multiple pages of your search results by clicking "settings" and changing it to 100 (default is 10) and save the preference. Every time you open a new browser session for search, you need to go through the same step.

Figure 3: Google search settings

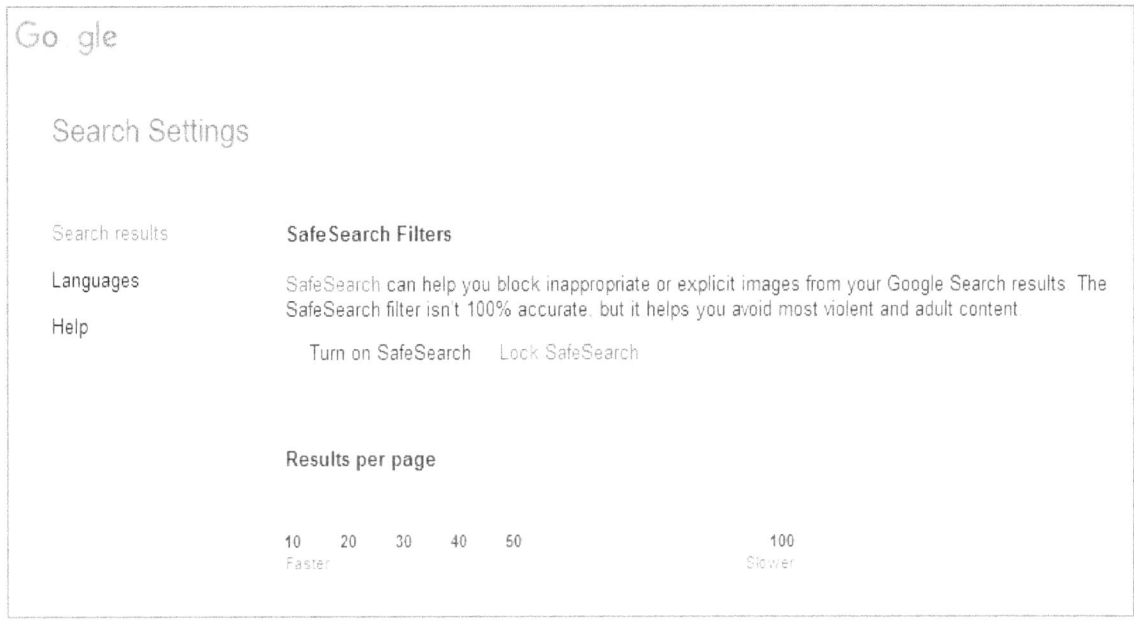

Tip 4: You can reduce the number of search results to a specific timeframe by year or by week or by providing a custom range.

Click "Tools" and you get the following menu

Figure 4: Google search settings

Click "Any time" and drop down menu with various options gets displayed

Figure 5: Google search settings

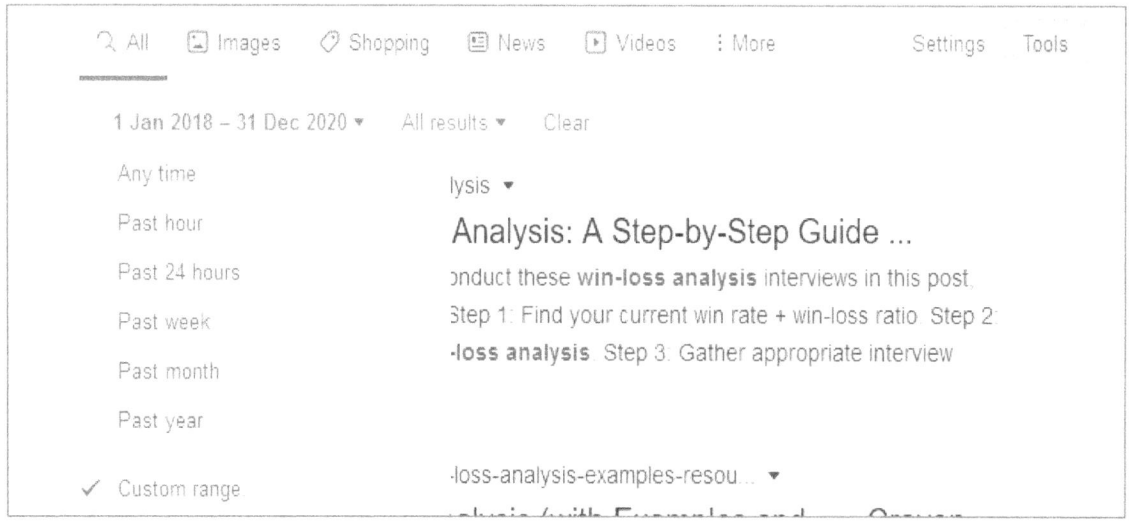

1.1 Inurl operator

inurl operator looks for information (i.e. "project manager, Bangalore as well as resume in the example below) present in the URL web page.

Example string: inurl:resume "project manager" Bangalore –job -jobs

Figure 6: inurl operator

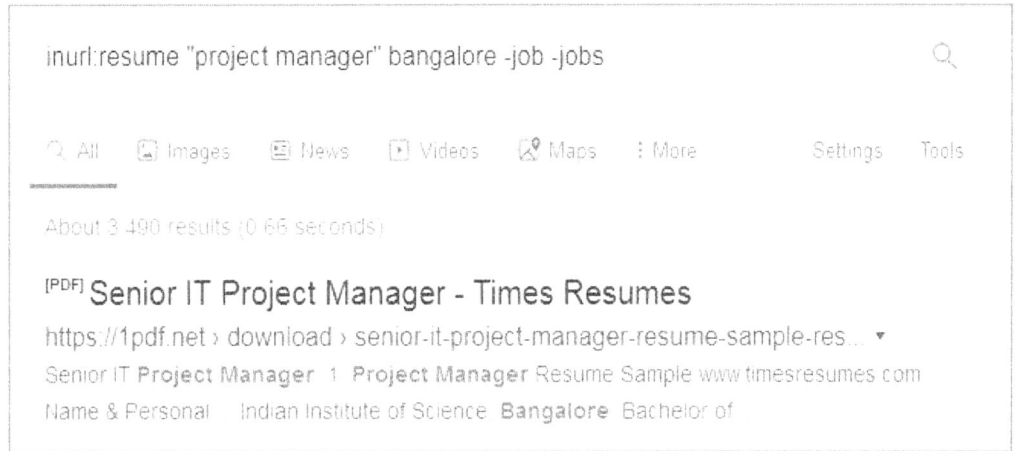

Likewise, you can utilize the inurl operator to search for specific topic as illustrated below:

Example string: inurl:bid management trends -jobs -construction

Figure 7: inurl operator usage

1.2 Intitle operator

The usage of intitle operator ensures that Google only returns the results where the searched terms are present in the meta title tag at the top of the page.

Example string: intitle:resume "bid manager" bangalore -job –jobs

Figure 8: intitle operator

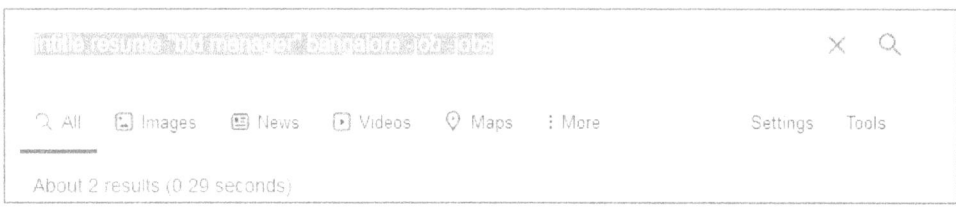

Likewise, you can utilize the intitle operator to search for specific topic as illustrated below:

Example string: intitle:"win loss analysis" (handbook OR guide OR cheatsheet OR primer)

Figure 9: intitle operator usage

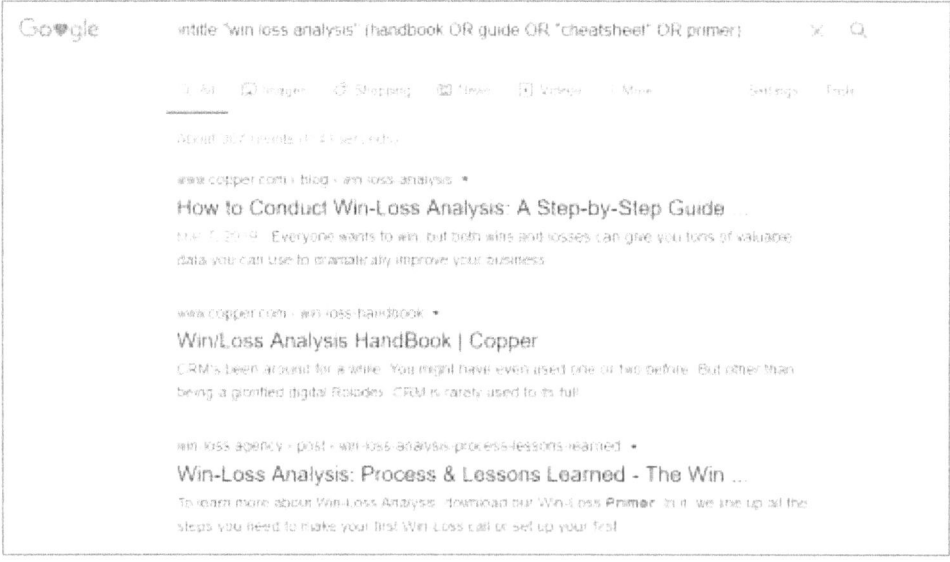

1.3 Intext operator

The intext operator returns results of web pages where the text of the searched term appears in the body of the page. If the searched term appears in the title but not in the body of the page, it will not provide that result.

You can utilize the intext operator to search for specific topic in the text of the web page as illustrated below:

Example string: intext:"win loss analysis" (handbook OR guide OR cheatsheet OR primer)

Figure 10: intext operator

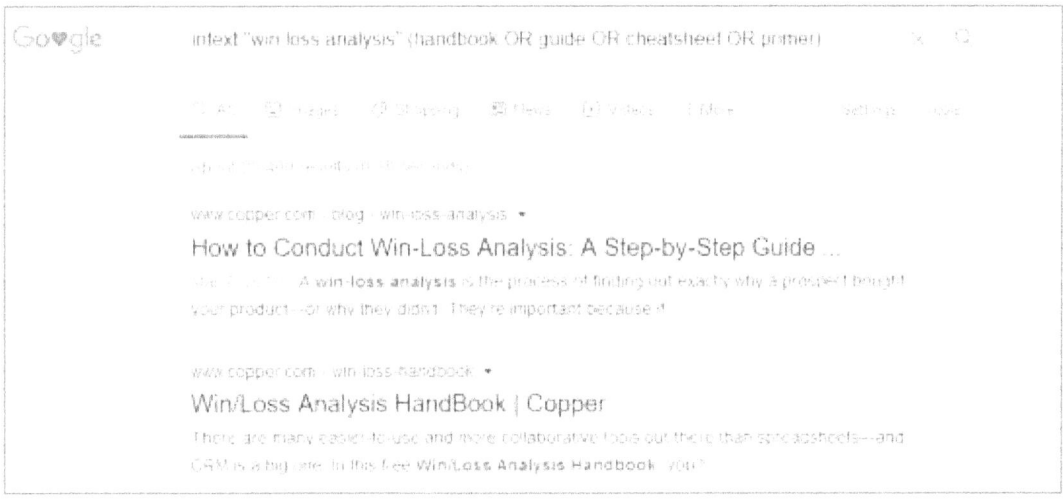

1.4 Related operator

"Related" operator gives you a list of the direct competitors as well as some peripheral competitors.

Figure 11: Related operator usage

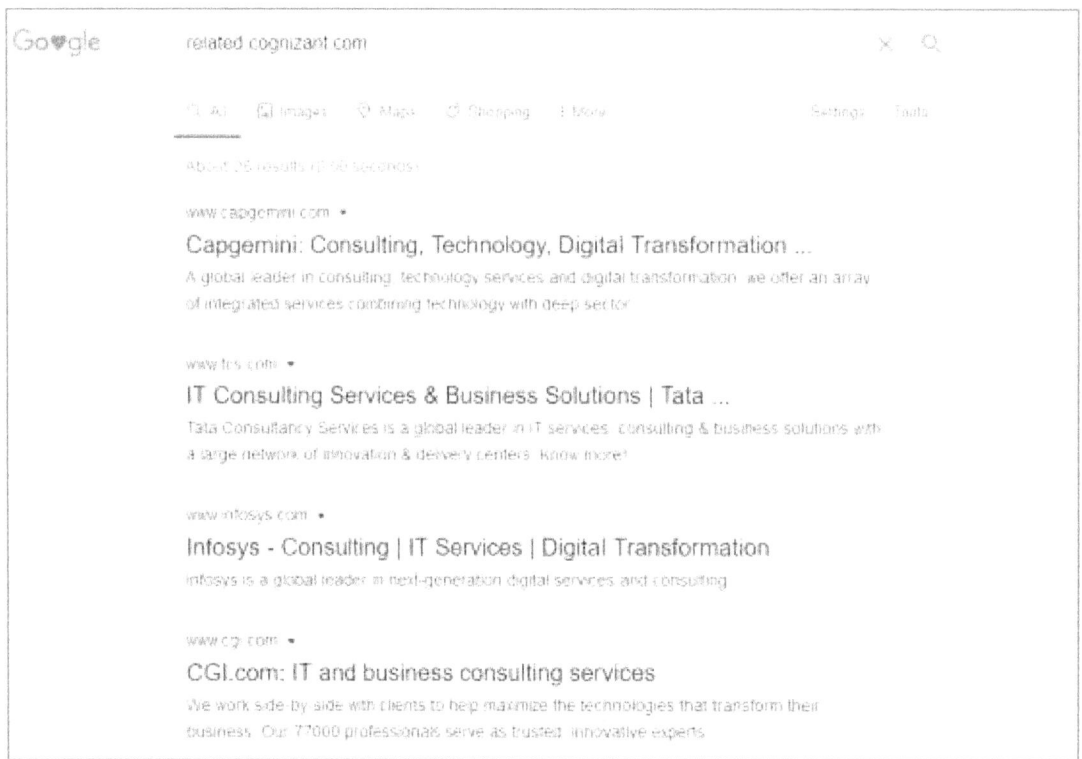

Caution:

Related operator is not always very reliable. A similar search for Deloitte.com did not list KPMG or EY as its competitors but listed only PWC. However, it can be used as a starting point for a competitor mapping exercise.

1.5 Filetype operator

You interact with a client and they are interested to work with you. You want to help them write the RFP but you may not have the specification document for that particular solution. Fret no more.

You can utilize the "filetype" syntax to find such documents if they have been uploaded, on the internet, as show in the example below.

String to use is:

filetype:pdf (RFP OR RFI OR RFQ OR Tender) "asset management"

There are several document formats like doc, docx, wpd that you can employ as well as part of your searches.

It's preferable not to combine multiple document formats into one string like below. Even though you seem like getting results, but if you were to review the results in detail, Google seems to ignore filetype operators other than the first one.

(filetype:pdf OR filetype:doc OR filetype:docx OR filetype:wpd OR filetype:RTF) (RFP OR RFI OR RFQ OR Tender) "asset management"

You can also use '**xls**' OR '**xlsx**' for excel based document retrieval or '**ppt, pptx**' for power point document retrieval.

Likewise you can find ps | odt | sxw | psw | pps extension files

Figure 12: filetype operator

You can utilize the filetype operator to find resumes or attendee lists that are publicly accessible only.

Example string to find resumes

filetype:pdf (inurl:resume OR intitle:resume) chicago -sample -example -"resume writing"

Example string to find attendee lists for a conference

filetype:xlsx conference "attendee list" -from -buy -scam -sponsor -form

1.6 Ext operator

There is an alternative operator to filetype called "**ext**" which gives identical results.

The search string to use is:

ext:pdf (RFP OR RFI OR RFQ OR Tender) "asset management"

Figure 13: ext operator

It is preferable not to combine multiple document formats like 'doc' or 'docx' or 'wpd' or 'RTF' in one string like below as many of these document formats may get ignored or inconsistent results can come about.

(ext:pdf OR ext:doc OR ext:docx OR ext:wpd OR ext:RTF) (RFP OR RFI OR RFQ OR Tender) "asset management"

1.7 AROUND (X) Operator

This search operator restricts the results to page links that contain search words within X words of each other.

This is useful in scenarios where you can cover all possible combinations of a certain specific word i.e. a job title or a School within few words of "company name" or "education" section in the resume as illustrated below:

Example string

developer AROUND (3) wipro (inurl:resume OR intitle:resume) -job -template -jobs -example

Figure 14: AROUND (X) operator

1.8 Number of words

The number of words that Google will execute is 32 maximum with a maximum of 128 characters per word. If you exceed it, Google ignores additional words.

1.9 Minus operator

If you are obtaining irrelevant results as part of your search, you can use the minus (-) sign to eliminate unwanted result links.

Some keywords to use after "-" sign are

- Job
- Jobs
- Example
- Examples
- Sample
- Template
- Topic
- Brochure
- Article
- "resume writing"
- Apply
- Submit

You can use other keywords based on your results to filter out unwanted results.

Chapter 2 Bing search engine

Google has a virtual monopoly in the search business but Bing from Microsoft is putting a lot of resources to make it a more effective search competitor.

Bing gives around 1000 available results for a search and has 2048 character search term limit.

Bing operator information

- filetype and ext operator for searching for documents works in a similar way as in Google.

- site operator works in a similar way as in Google for X-ray of a website

- inanchor operator returns web pages that contain the specified term in the anchor text of any links in the indexed pages

- inbody operator returns web pages that contain the specified term in the metadata of the page content

- intitle operator returns web pages that contain the specified term in the title of the site

- INSTREAMSET operator can be used to search the Title, URL, Body, and Anchors of a page by inserting each term into the second section of the operator.

- location or loc operator returns webpages from a specific country or region (ex: loc::US OR loc:in)

- near operator looks for specific words within a certain distance (example: mansion near:5 california)

- site/domain shall limit the search to a particular root domain like .org, .eu, .gov, .edu (example: "IT security" site/.gov)

Following are some of the search strings you can utilize for your requirements:

Example 1: This string will search for CV (as well as its synonyms "Resume" and "Curriculum Vitae") of Account manager in Delhi in title or URL of a web page

instreamset:(title url):cv "account manager" Delhi -jobs -sample -apply -template –submit

OR (the same search as above but will search title or anchor of a web page)

instreamset:(title anchor):cv "account manager" Delhi -jobs -sample -apply -template –submit

Example 2: This string does an X-ray of Linkedin and looks for sales enablement skillset in Bangalore.

site:in.linkedin.com/in ("location:Bangalore" OR "location:Bengaluru area") "sales enablement" Cloud -recruiter

The above string, simplified as below, churns out even more results..

site:in.linkedin.com/in "bengaluru area, india" "sales enablement" Cloud -recruiter

Example 3: Research companies in Bengaluru in software industry

site:in.linkedin.com/company inbody:software bengaluru

Example 4: Finding CTO of Walmart, for executive mapping purposes

site:linkedin.com/in intitle:walmart intitle:CTO

Chapter 3 Linkedin

Linkedin has become the leading social media platform for business lead generation, talent mapping, competitive insights and communication.

Linkedin public profiles are stored in "in" and "pub" directories. Nowadays they are more stored in "in" directories only.

A simple native linkedin search can be executed like this:

Figure 15: Linkedin native search

The results of the above search provides the following menu.

Figure 16: Linkedin native search

Once you click "people" sub-menu, here is the end-result

You can then choose "companies" Tab to select "current company" and/or "locations" tab to select the desired location..

Figure 17: Linkedin native search

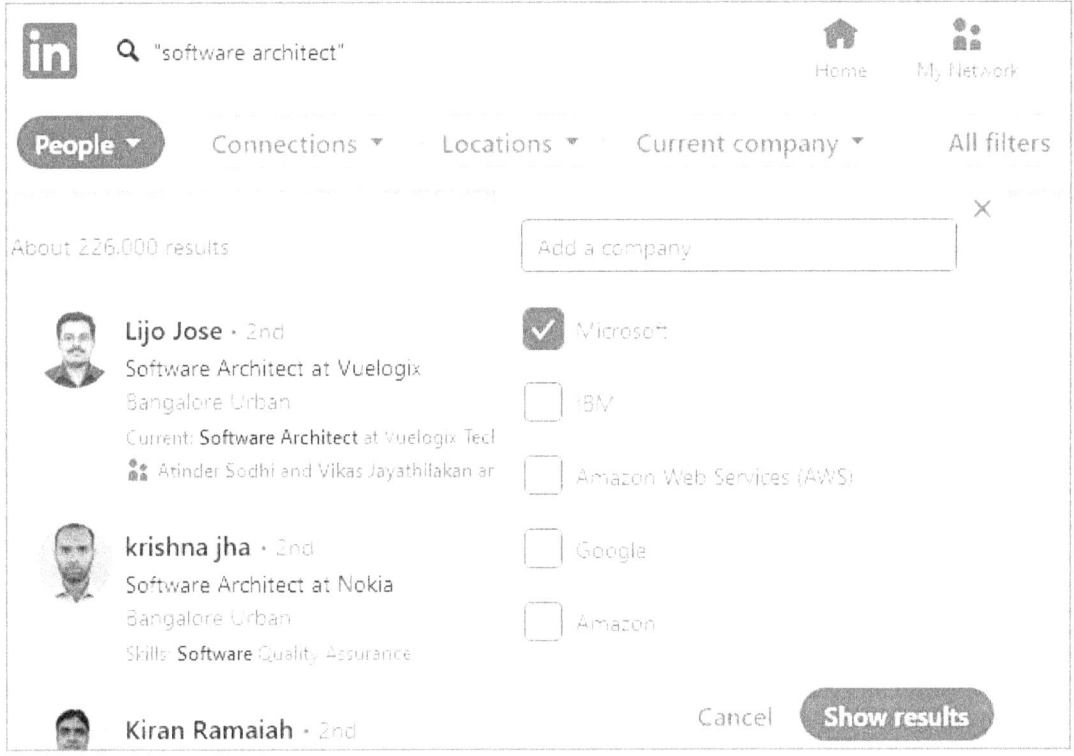

3.1 Linkedin X-ray

Linkedin restricts the number of profiles one can view using their "Free" account.

You can however search Linkedin through Google by using the site operator.

Basic X-ray search would be site:linkedin.com/in

An example string to use is site:linkedin.com/in ("proposal manager" OR "bid manager") Boston

Figure 18: Linkedin X-ray

You can use the filetype operator targeting a specific site like this:

filetype:pdf (RFP OR RFI OR RFQ OR Tender) "asset management" .gov

Likewise you can utilize the filetype operator to look for 'doc' or 'docx' or 'wpd' or 'RTF" based document formats.

Replace .gov with any other domain name to get specific results. Replace .gov with .gov.in to obtain India specific results

You can filter the profiles based on number of years of experience as illustrated below (Note: This will only show candidates who have mentioned years of experience in their profile)

site:linkedin.com/in "program manager" Chicago ("11 OR 12 OR 13 OR 14 OR 15 years of experience")

OR

site:linkedin.com/in ("over 10" | "over 11" | "over 12" | "10+" | "11+" | "12+") "program manager" Chicago area

3.2 Country code filter

You can filter Linkedin results by two letter country code. Illustration of UK search filter is shown below:

Figure 19: Linkedin country code usage (UK)

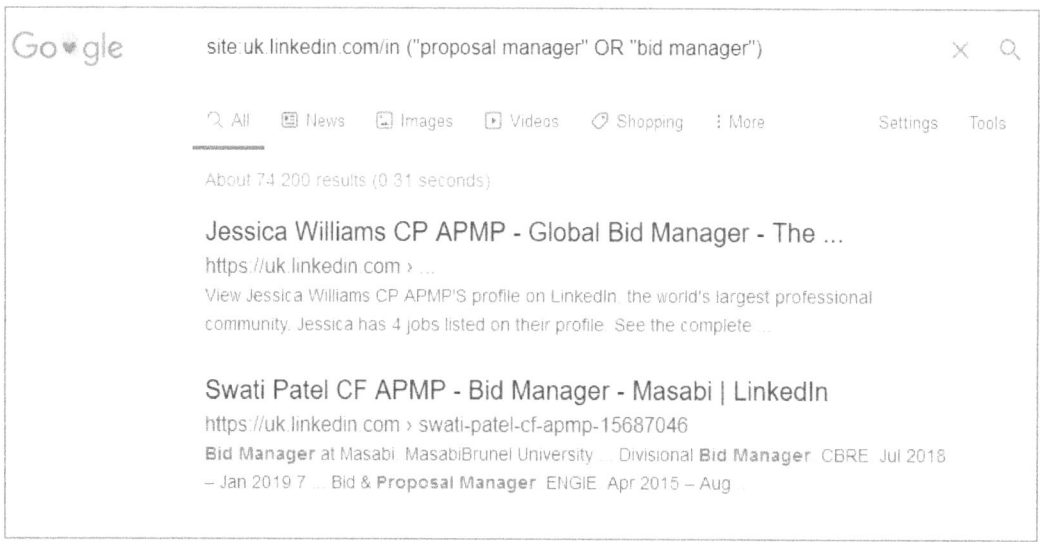

Replace "uk" with another country code (2 characters) to obtain the desired country profiles.

3.3 Linkedin country codes

Following URL provides the list of country codes for Linkedin

https://www.globalrecruitingroundtable.com/2011/04/08/list-of-countries-on-linkedin-incl-code/

3.4 Feed search

You can also search the feed of Linkedin as illustrated below:

Figure 20: Linkedin Feed search

Figure 21: Linkedin Feed search

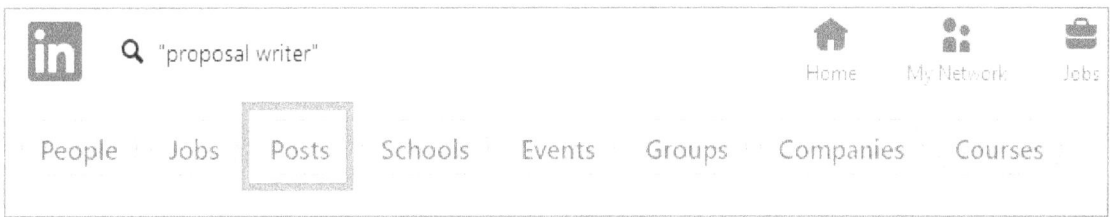

Figure 22: Linkedin Feed search

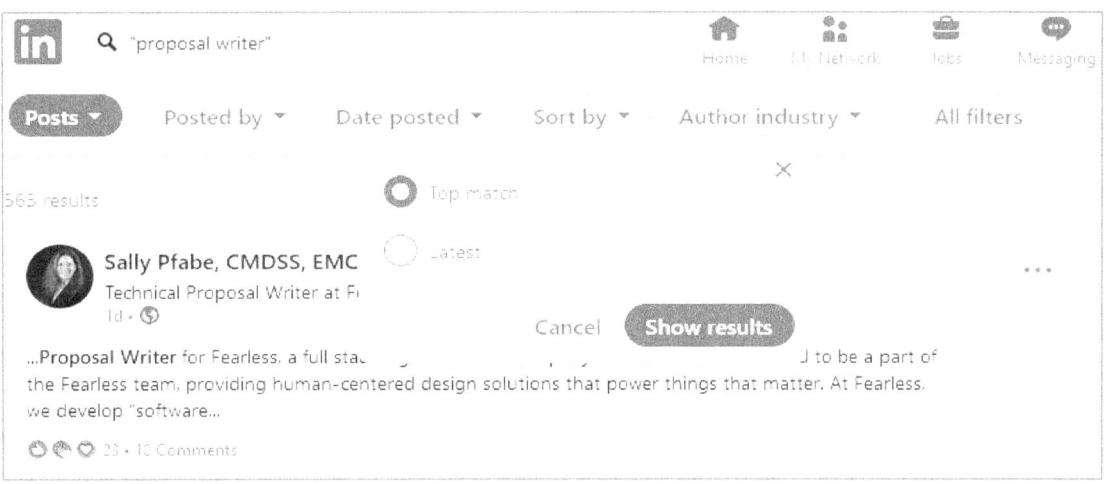

3.5 Certification search

Linkedin feeds provide several updates in so many areas of interest. One update which caught my attention is the certification achievement status.

Eg: A **("verified achievement" salesforce)** search in Linkedin search box filtered on "content" basis lists all the individuals with specific certifications as illustrated below:

Figure 23: Linkedin Feed certification Search

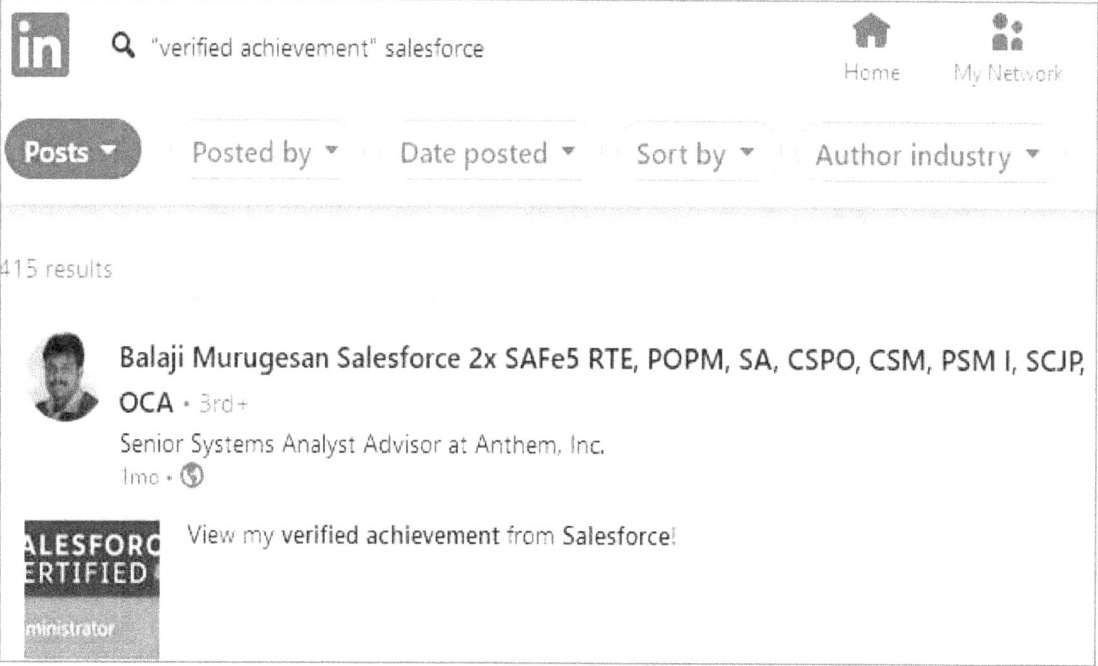

Search string to find people with APMP badges from "Acclaim"

Acclaim is a certification agency from which individuals can pass an exam and upload their certifications on Linkedin.

site:youracclaim.com/users APMP

An often ignored option to search for relevant profiles is Credentials. Nowadays, there are a lot of courses available on demand and you can search whether an individual has completed a specific certification by using the following term in Linkedin search box and click the "Posts" Tab" for the results

APMG ("Certificate of completion") APMP

(APMG is the issuing authority)

Likewise a simple search of **"credential ID" salesforce** in the Linkedin search box gives relevant skill certification results

Tip 5: If you notice a competitor's or client's key employees taking such courses or finished such courses, it can be a signal to you that the employee maybe leaving the organization or the organization has upcoming projects on specific technologies or products that you can leverage.

3.6 Linkedin groups

An under-utilized source of information, reviews and interaction is Linkedin Groups.

Following are some groups which may be of some interest. Linkedin Login maybe required.

https://www.linkedin.com/groups/59418/ - Bid and Proposal management professionals

https://www.linkedin.com/groups/4048421/ - Bids, Tenders, International Business Proposal Writing, Bid Management, Global Sales, & Tendering

https://www.linkedin.com/groups/12101608/ - Women in bids and proposals

https://www.linkedin.com/groups/42114/ - APMP Official discussion group

https://www.linkedin.com/groups/12204882/ - APMP India

Example illustration of finding "women in bids and proposals" within Linkedin groups without being a member of a group. Sounds cool isn't it? This will not pull all the member lists but quite a few.

site:linkedin.com/in "women in bids and proposals" -job -career -recruiter -recruitment -talent

Just replace the group name within the quotes as well as the location names to find professionals in another group.

3.7 Linkedin email address search

Some Linkedin members display their email address publicly and here is the example search string to find it

site:linkedin.com/in ("gmail.com" OR "yahoo.com" OR "hotmail.com" OR "icloud.com") chennai "proposal writer" –recruiter

site:ca.linkedin.com/in ("gmail.com" OR "yahoo.com" OR "hotmail.com" OR "icloud.com" OR "@shaw.ca" OR "@rogers.com" OR "@videotron.ca" OR "bell.net") ("proposal writer" OR "bid manager")

(For Canada based email addresses lookup)

3.8 Personal branding

From a personal branding perspective, Linkedin has a few quirky features that you would want to be aware of:

While posting there, avoid using more than three Hash tags as it seems to limit the reach of your posting.

How to find out which Hash tags have the most followers?

There is no easy way to do it. In the later part of 2019, Andy Foote was compiling a list of Top 100 Linkedin Hash tags followers and I uncovered a few of them like #innovation, #future, #futurism, #professionalwomen, #personalbranding that he could add into his comprehensive list.

Figure 24: Linkedin Hash tag

Relevant hash tags for bid management professionals:

- #APMP
- #Proposalwriting
- #proposals
- #proposalmanagement
- #bids
- #bidmanagement
- #bidwriting
- #bidding
- #bidmanager
- #bidstream

Some topic related interesting hash tags you can explore are:

- #hiringandpromotion
- #cloudcomputing
- #mobileapplications
- #mobiletechnology
- #ecommerce
- #design
- #data
- #datamining
- #softwaredesign

Guess which country hash tag has the most followers?

- #India which has close to 68 Million followers
- The key is not to spam these tags too much.

If you need to know which hash tag has how many followers, just type #hashtagname (replace "hash tag name" with data for example to find how many followers are there for #data hash tag) in the Linkedin search bar on the top left corner and click the result, you will see the number.

Just because a certain hash tag has lesser number of followers, does not mean that you have to sideline it. Look it up and see if it has a lot of engagement from participants.

For example **#APMP** (for bid managers and proposal writers) has few followers but it is a very good hash tag for very bid management specific content distribution and marketing.

Once you post a hash tag in your post and even if you replace an existing tag, it is pointless as it does not give any reach at all.

Create your own hash tag like I did with **#byteizelearn** to increase your personal branding

Chapter 4 Sourcing tools

There are hundreds of Paid sourcing tools available and new ones keep cropping up all the time. They are only our assistants in the end to improve your productivity, so that you can spend more time talking to candidates to know their motivations, their growth plans etc.

Some prominent chrome extension tools are:

- Hiretual – It's a very good tool to find candidates along with their contact information. It collates the information from Linkedin, and other social media platforms.

- Amazinghiring - It's also a very good tool to find candidates along with their contact information. It collates the information from Linkedin, and other social media platforms.

- Seekout – A talent and labour market intelligence solution. It collates the candidate information from Linkedin and other social media platforms and presents it in an easy to use format with several filters and can also provide contact information.

- Swordfish – Find cellphone numbers and email addresses

- Signalhire – Email and phone number finder

Free contact look up tools

https://Canada411.ca

https://www.melissa.com/v2/lookups/

Caution:

Test the Paid tools during the trial period and then decide on purchasing them

Please obtain the clearance from IT security team before installing chrome extension tools on your work computer. Some of them may have spyware or ransom ware hidden inside.

4.1 Free corporate email address search tool

A sales professional finds a prospect's name and maybe if they are lucky, they may get an email address (Corporate or personal). More often than not, email addresses are unavailable for a majority of the prospects. Corporate email addresses come with a myriad number of combinations.

One option to find a person's corporate email address is
https://cultivatedculture.com/mailscoop/

All you need is the person's name, company website address and voila, you get the email.

Figure 25: Finding an individual's email

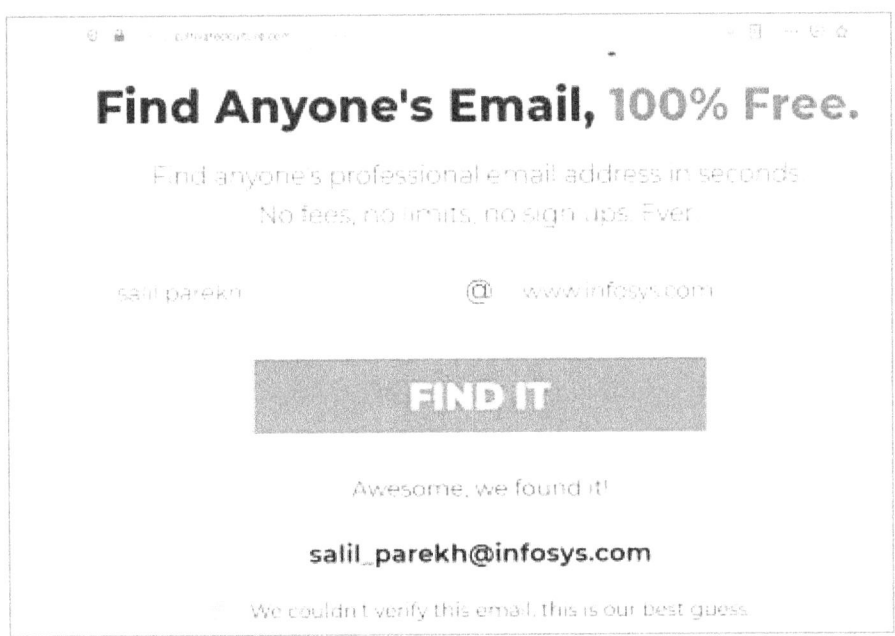

There are a lot of free (with limited credits) and paid personal email finder tools available in the market.

A productivity trick to find emails through Outlook.com

You may have an email address but want to know the Linkedin profile of the individual.

Open a free outlook account at outlook.live.com and use that email address as a login email to Linkedin as illustrated below:

Login to your Free outlook email account and click "switch to people" highlighted in "Green" and then click "New contact".

Figure 26: Outlook.live.com email

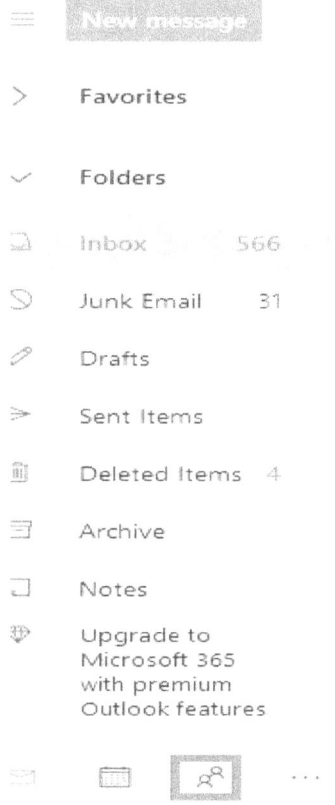

If the added contact has a Linkedin account, the Linkedin profile is displayed right away as illustrated below:

Figure 27: Linkedin contact display in Outlook

(information has been scrubbed)

4.2 Validating an email address

While we somehow may find an email address, there are ways to check whether it is a valid and functioning email.

Following are a few free tools to check whether it's a valid email address:

Hunter.io

Email Checker

VerifyEmail

VerifyEmailAddress

Verifalia

This reduces the chances of email bouncing and saving your precious time.

4.3 Prospect email engagement

We may derive great happiness in finding the contact information i.e. email address of a prospect. The bigger issue is to know whether the prospect has even opened the email, if so, when and if they have clicked any attachments and how many times. There are tools for that too.

Following are couple of tools that you can evaluate to see if they are a right fit for the type of work you are undertaking.

Hubspot – It has a free CRM component but has a paid subscription for lead generation, email tracking, scheduling and marketing automation.

Docsify is a Gmail Chrome extension (Trial period of 1-2 weeks) which lets you know:

- When and how many times recipients opened emails
- Know the geo-location and device type of your recipients
- Get a real-time notification when recipients open emails
- File tracking

4.4 Outreach management

Now that you have the email address, you would need to create a proper outreach message, to ascertain the interest level and drive further engagement.

The subject line can make or break the conversation. What words will capture a prospect's attention?

A good tool to check is sendcheckit.com which allows you to do subject line testing. It is a good indicator of what might interest a prospect but do a lot of A/B testing to get it right though and not rely 100% on such tools to make a decision.

Example: "RPA audit". It gives a reading comprehension level of "second grade" better than eighth grade, no spam words, sentiment analysis of Zero and has only 8 characters for mobile device reading, again an excellent metric.

Figure 28: Sendcheckit.com

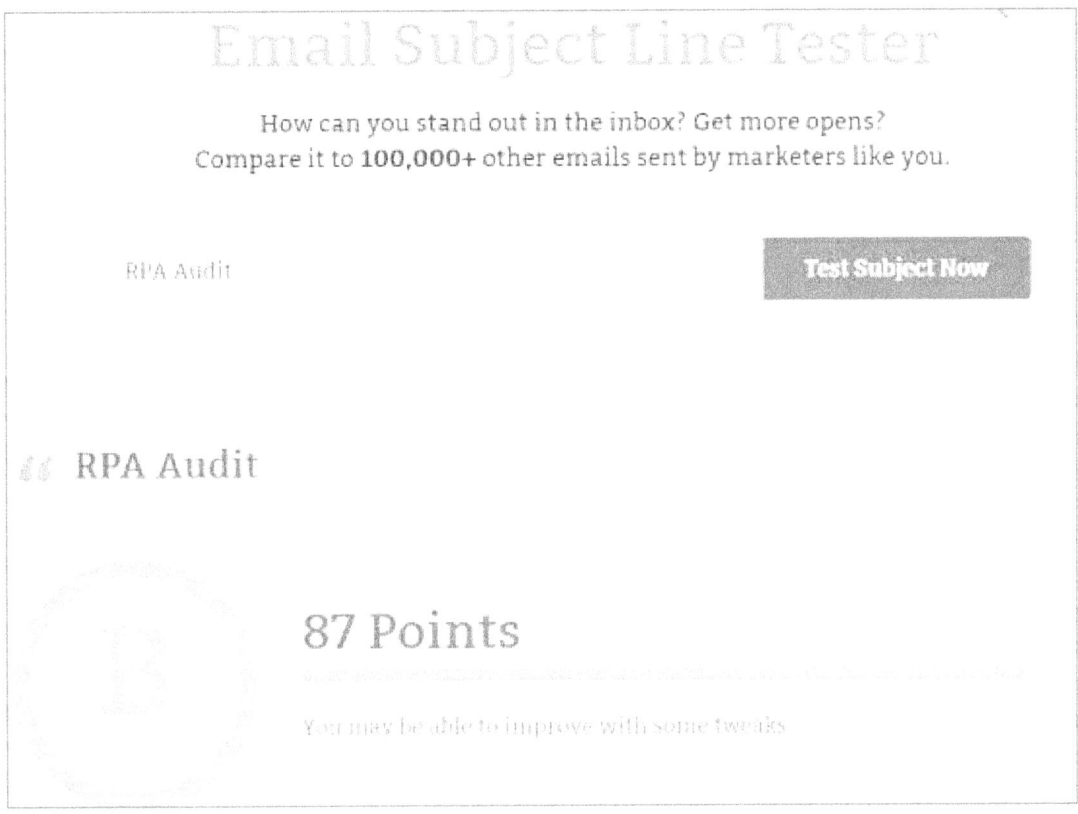

Figure 29: Sendcheckit.com

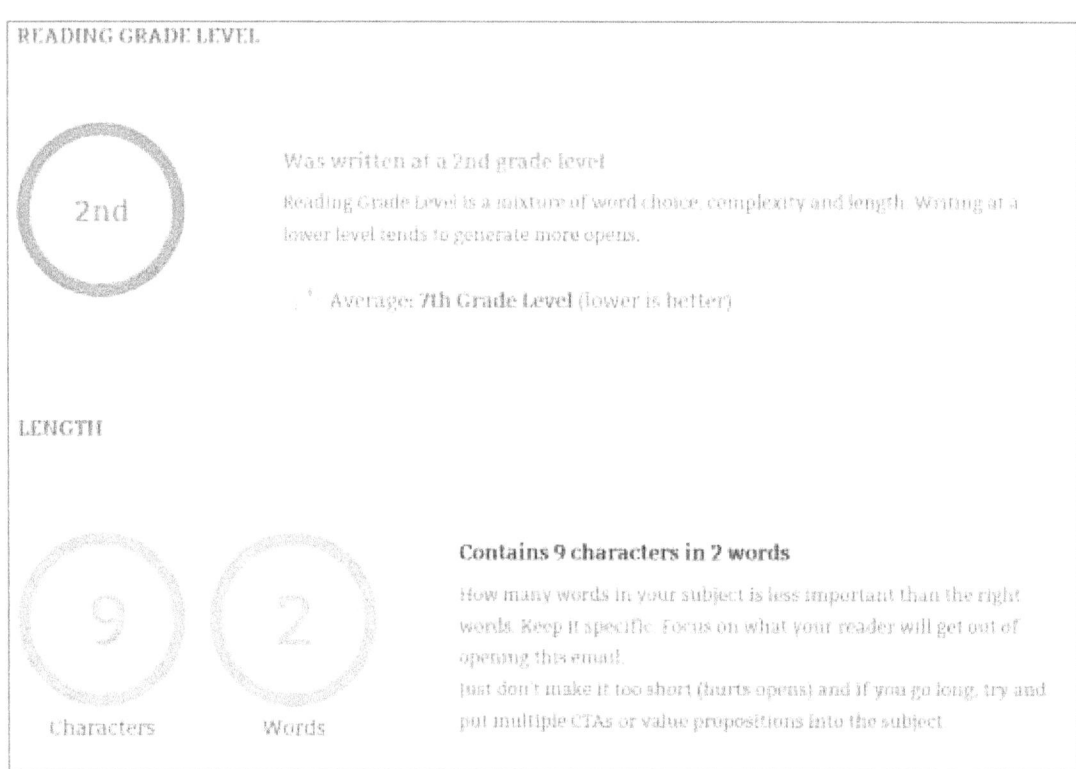

Figure 30: sendcheckit.com

4.5 Tool for Notes and timestamps for Google search

How many times we wished there was a way to keep track of a website we visited or a Linkedin profile and maybe add a note about it? Now it's possible.

WhenX is an excellent Chrome extension tool that boosts your productivity by embedding a note about a web page to the page itself enables you to differentiate between search results you already know from past searches. The days of searching through Browser history can be put to rest as it adds a timestamp for every specific web link you browse.

For Recruiters & Sales people, it allows you to create a note on any Linkedin profile, make a note, using the default lead status option

Chapter 5 Twitter

Twitter is an excellent avenue to obtain latest events, news as well as analyzing competitor moves. Since digital transformation is a booming area, a lot of useful information can be gleaned.

Here is an illustration of how it can be used effectively:

You need to have a twitter account for a start. I typed in her name as illustrated below in the search bar on the top right hand corner. A feed of her posts below her profile come about. You can follow her as well.

Figure 31: Twitter followers

One of her tweets referred to "Oslo business forum". Turns out they have an event in the later part of 2020 where Steve Wozniak, Seth Godin are the prominent speakers.

Figure 32: Twitter events reference

One of her other tweets referred to "Oslo Big Data Day". Turns out they have an event in the later part of 2020 where there are a lot of industry relevant speakers that are slated to present.

Figure 33: Twitter events notification

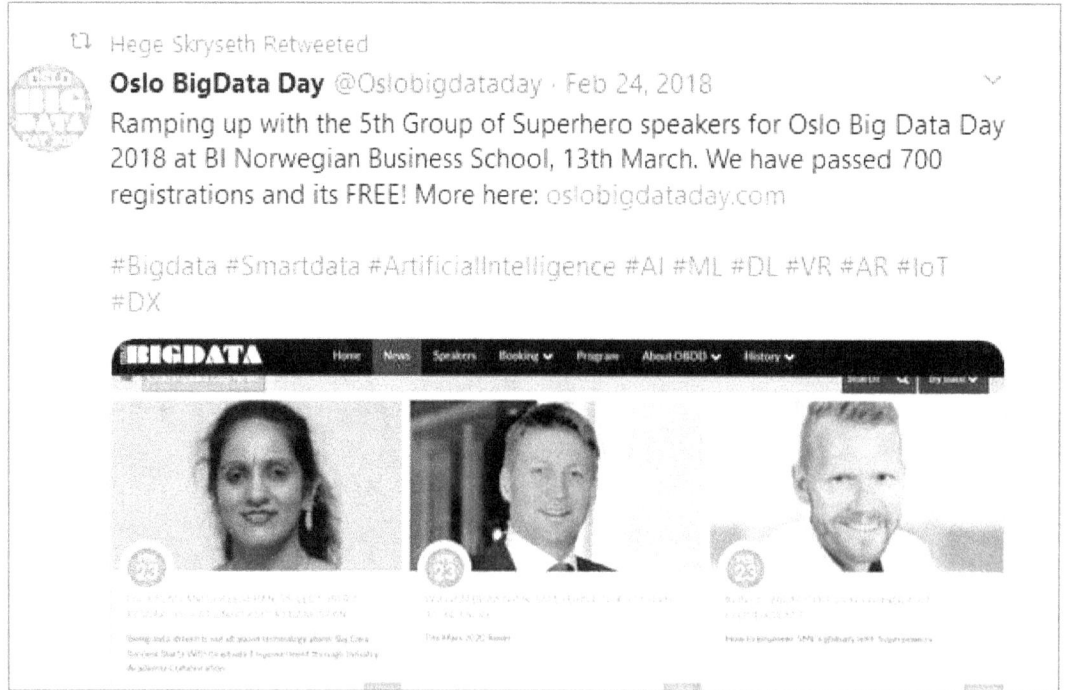

Figure 34: Competitor presence

Look at the highlighted competitors who are associate partners for this event.

5.1 Twitter X-ray

You can search tweets using the following strings:

In Google

site:twitter.com "azure architect" bangalore -job -jobs –careers

There are quite a few chief digital officers on Twitter. You can search by name or by using a term "Chief digital officer" as illustrated below and follow them to get the latest updates from these individuals. The twitter feeds contain videos as well which you can review to see if there is any valuable information.

Also do check www.cdoclub.com which gives a good overview of who joined as a new CDO and if you subscribe to the Jobs, you would also notice which companies are looking to hire a new CDO

.Figure 35:   Twitter native search

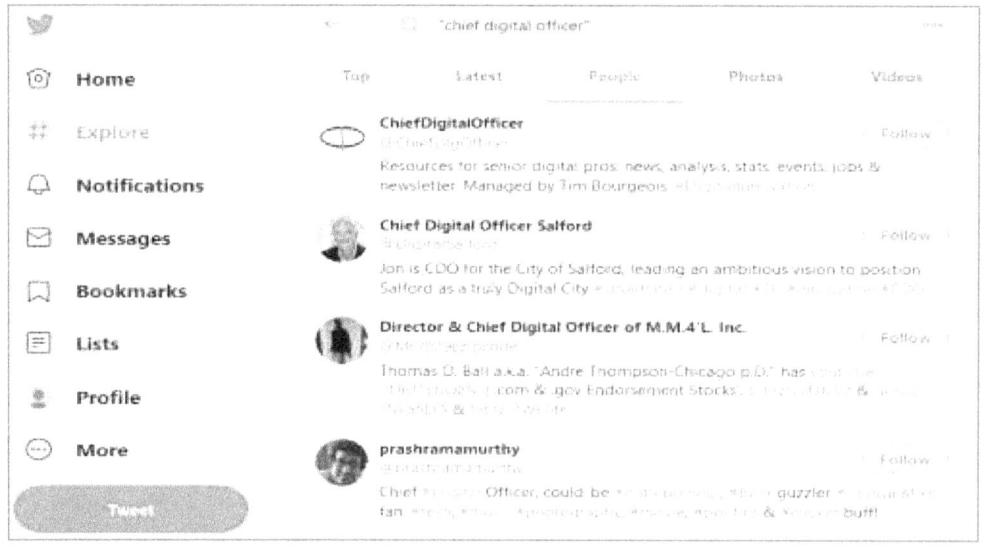

You can check the identity of the followers for a specific Twitter handle, which may be of some importance.

Example: **@cioreview**

Figure 36: CIOReview magazine twitter handle

Click "**the15.3k followers**" to reveal the individuals who are following CIOReview. If you find anyone interesting, you can click "Follow" and get their updates in your feed. You can also see who you may know might be following them. ("Followers you know" Tab).

Figure 37: CIOReview Twitter handle followers

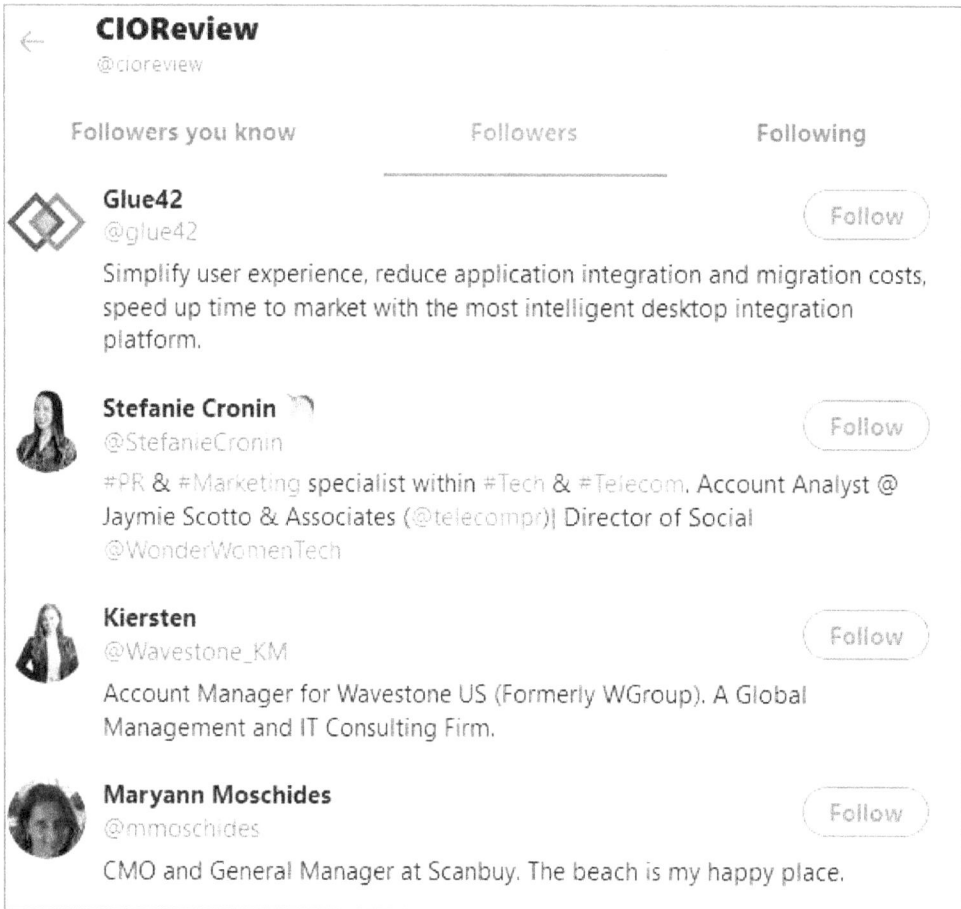

Chapter 6 Facebook

Facebook is the largest social network in the world. It has more than 2.5 billion profiles and also hosts a lot of interest groups that could be a valuable source of information. Some users restrict their profiles to their friends or family circle, so some public information may not be available to review.

6.1 Facebook X-ray search

Sample X-ray of Facebook strings that you can execute which will reveal candidate profiles are as follows:

site:facebook.com "profile photo" "pre sales specialist" Toronto, Ontario

site:facebook.com "profile photo" "pursuit lead"

site:facebook.com "Join Facebook to connect with" "sales specialist" Bangalore

6.2 Facebook native search

There are thousands of Facebook groups for every interest (Professional or personal) that one can think of. The Native search options are limitless.

An example illustration of a "Salesforce" professional interest group search is as follows. There are technical forums, jobs, recruiting groups.

Figure 38: Facebook groups

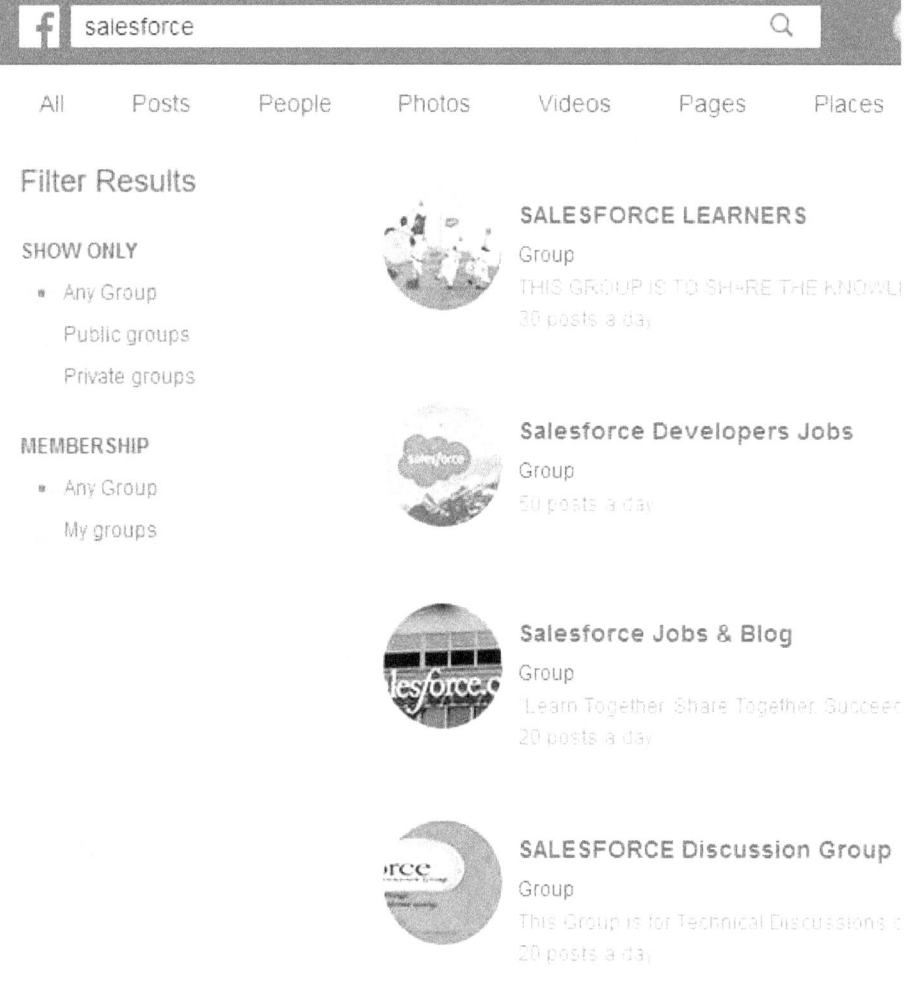

You can X-ray Facebook to find groups. An example of searching for groups related to Microsoft is illustrated below:

site:facebook.com inurl:groups intitle:microsoft

Figure 39: Facebook X-ray

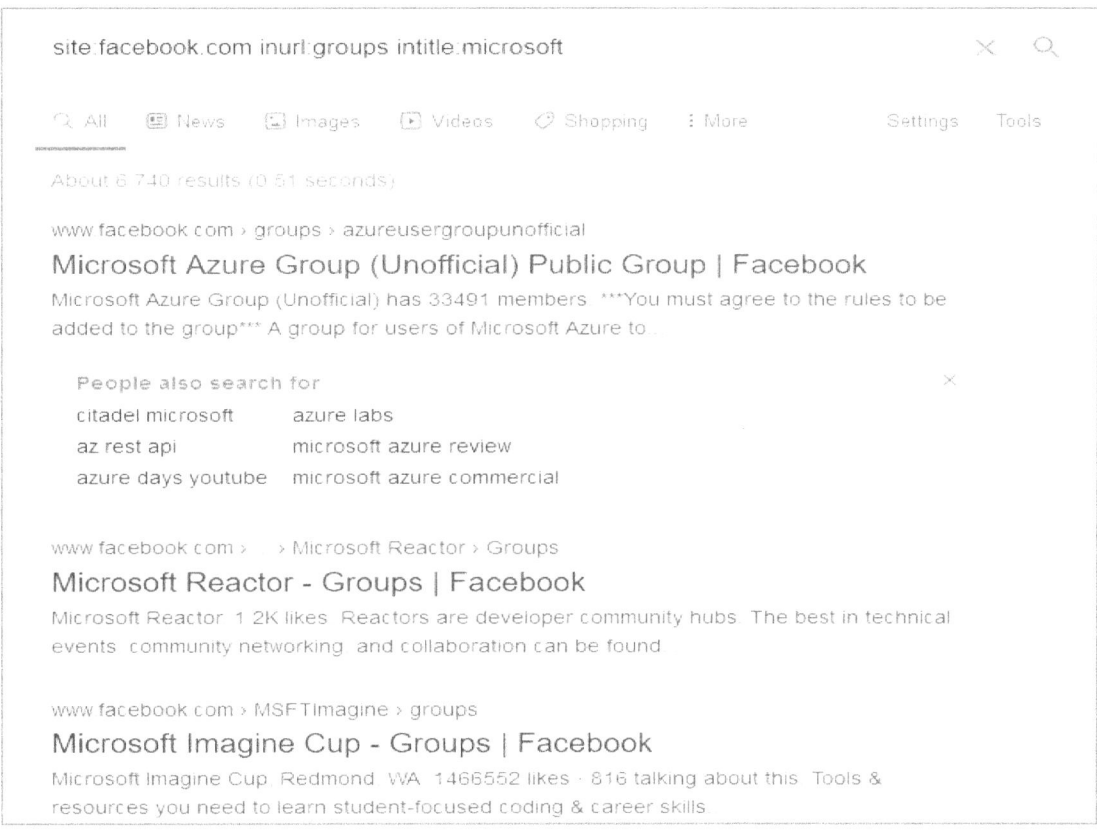

Chapter 7 Competitive Intelligence

Competitive intelligence (CI) can be useful to map current and emerging competitor's organization structures, compensation and benefit trends, competitor team structures, career growth parameters etc. For CI information to be put into action, excellent relationship with stakeholders needs to be maintained.

Competitive intelligence can take the shape of many ways and there are two sources of information gathering.

Primary Sources

- External buyers
- Suppliers
- Partners
- Research agencies
- Competitor staff at trade shows, events
- Internal company sales, engineering and R&D teams

Secondary Sources

- Social media
- Competitor websites
- News releases
- Patent and trademark sites
- Employer rating sites etc.

7.1 X-raying a site

Using the site operator, you can x-ray almost any website. An example is shown below for executive mapping purposes.

site:linkedin.com/in intitle:CTO intitle:Walmart

(Spaces before intitle)

The above string provides the results of CTO currently working at Walmart

Figure 40: Linkedin X-ray

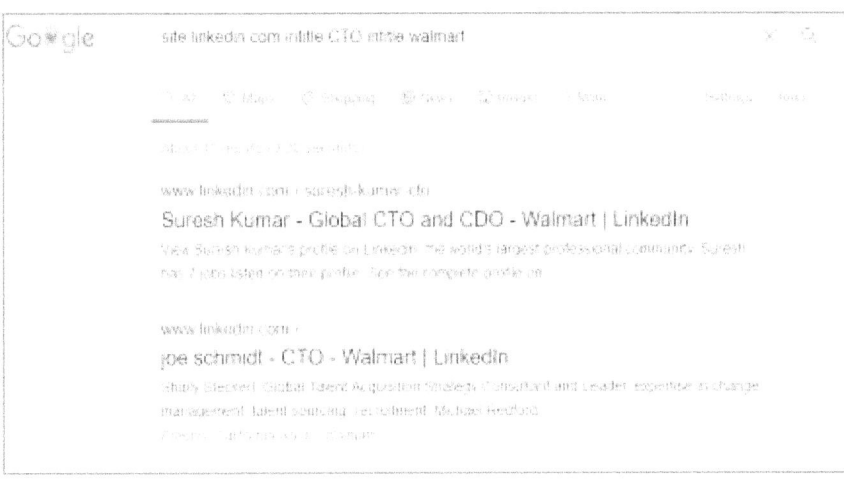

7.2 Techcrunch and Crunchbase

Techcrunch primarily reports on the business related to tech, technology news, analysis of emerging trends in tech, and profiling of new tech businesses and products

Example search strings you could employ are as illustrated below:

site:techcrunch.com "walmart" (VP OR director)   OR

site:techcrunch.com "funding" bangalore

Crunchbase is a platform for finding business information about private and public companies. Crunchbase information includes investments and funding information, founding members and individuals in leadership positions, mergers and acquisitions, news, and industry trends.

7.3 Newspaper and Financial magazine sites

A gem hidden in plain sight is New York Times or Bloomberg

You can track executive moves by using very simple string as follows:

site:nytimes.com (CEO OR CFO) (joining OR hired OR stepping OR replaced OR leaving OR resign) "walmart"

site:bloomberg.com/ (CEO OR CFO) (joining OR hired OR stepping OR replaced OR leaving OR resign) "walmart"

*Substitute "Walmart" with the desired name of the firm to get the actual results

7.4 Government planning departments

When companies are expanding their current offices or opening new offices in town, they will be filing their applications with the town or county or city planning offices for real estate and other permits much ahead of any press releases. Do keep an eye on local planning departments.

7.5 Patent, Technical db and Research publications search

A search of a competitor's publicly available patent portfolio databases can give an insight in to the products development strategy, their depth and breadth of commitment to R&D. This will help in predicting the market orientation and plug gaps in your IP portfolio and be adequately prepared for market disruption.

Following are some of the avenues to look up such information:

European Patent Registry search

US Patent and Trademark Office

Canadian Patent Database

Google patent search

7.5.1 Google scholar

Google Scholar provides a simple way to broadly search for scholarly literature. From one place, you can search across many disciplines and sources: articles, theses, books, abstracts and court opinions, from academic publishers, professional societies, online repositories, universities and other web sites.

You can filter the results by date or year or to include patents or citations. However, the results need to be cross-referenced with Linkedin or other sources to confirm the right profile.

Figure 41: Google Scholar

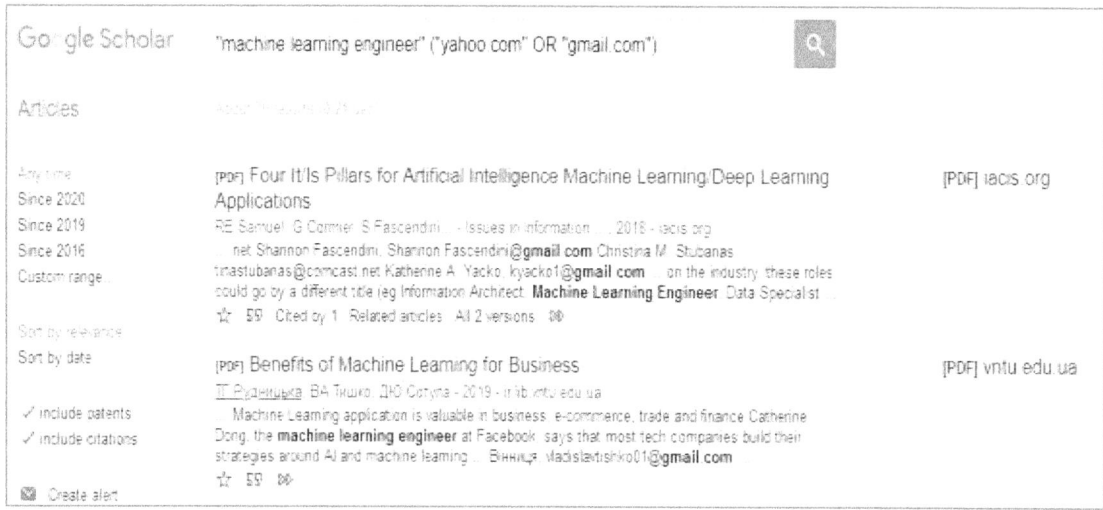

Surprisingly an X-Ray search is way more effective in neatly arranging the results by an individual name as illustrated below:

site:scholar.google.com "machine learning" retail

Figure 42: Google Scholar X-ray

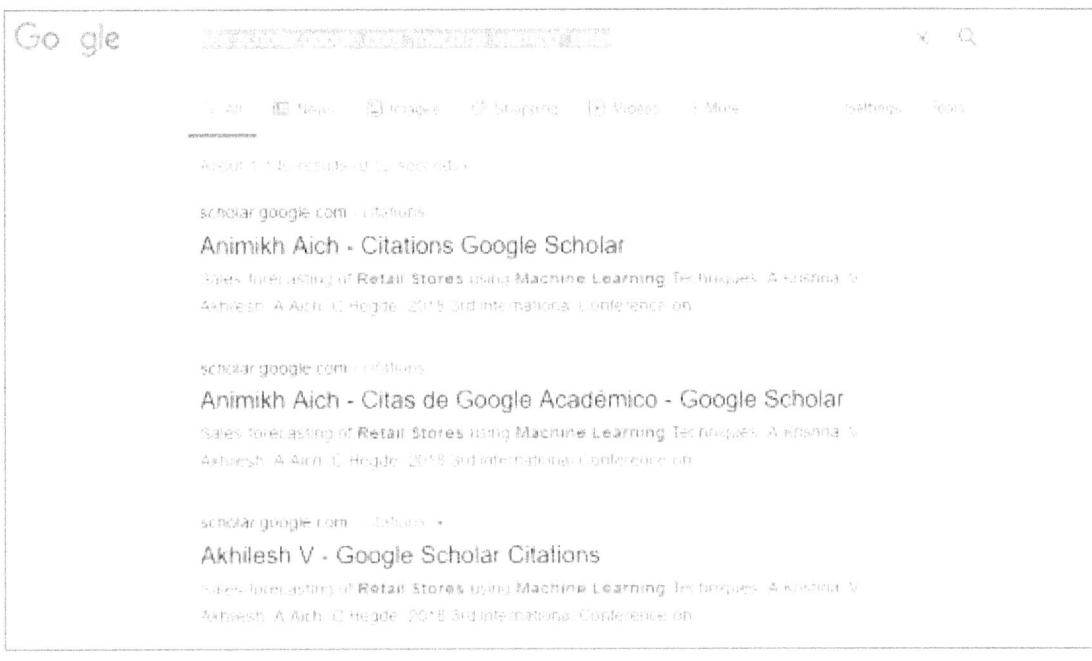

7.5.2 Microsoft Academic

Microsoft Academic is an impressive search facility available to find articles, citations, abstracts etc. from 1978 onwards as illustrated below:

Figure 43: Microsoft Academic

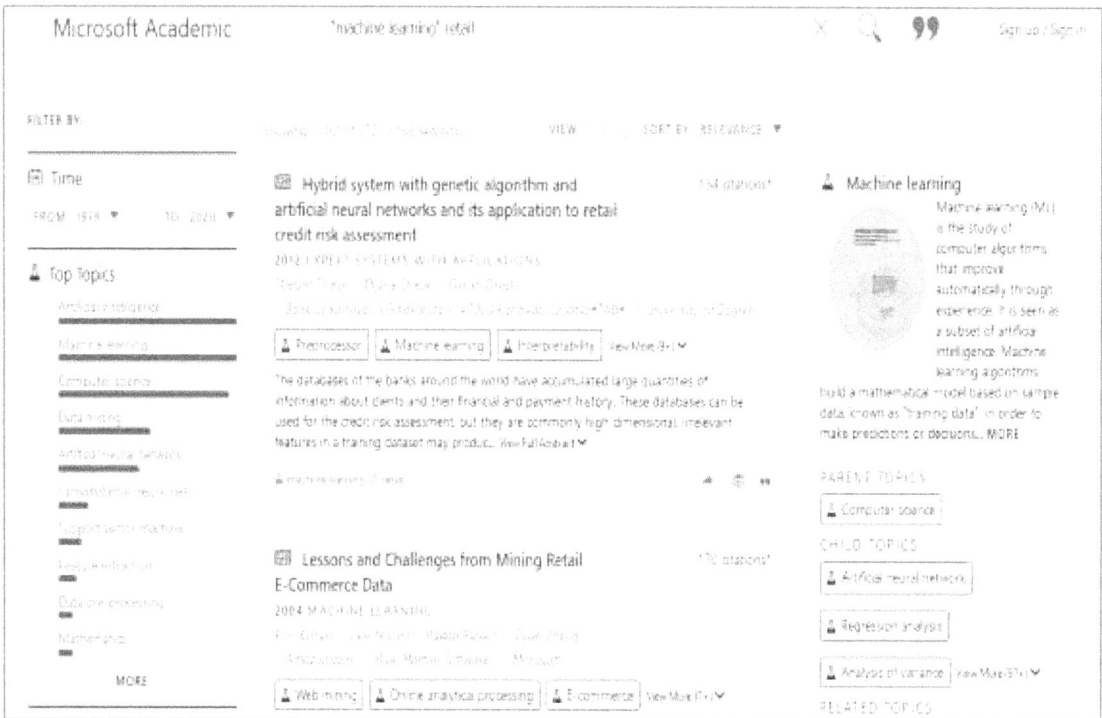

It can be x-rayed as illustrated below:

site:academic.microsoft.com "machine learning" retail

7.5.3 Semantic Scholar

Semantic Scholar is a relatively new AI academic research tool that finds hidden connections and links between research topics.

It can be x-rayed as well for example like this:

site:semanticscholar.org "machine learning" retail

site:pdfs.semanticscholar.org "machine learning" retail

Figure: 44 - Semantic Scholar

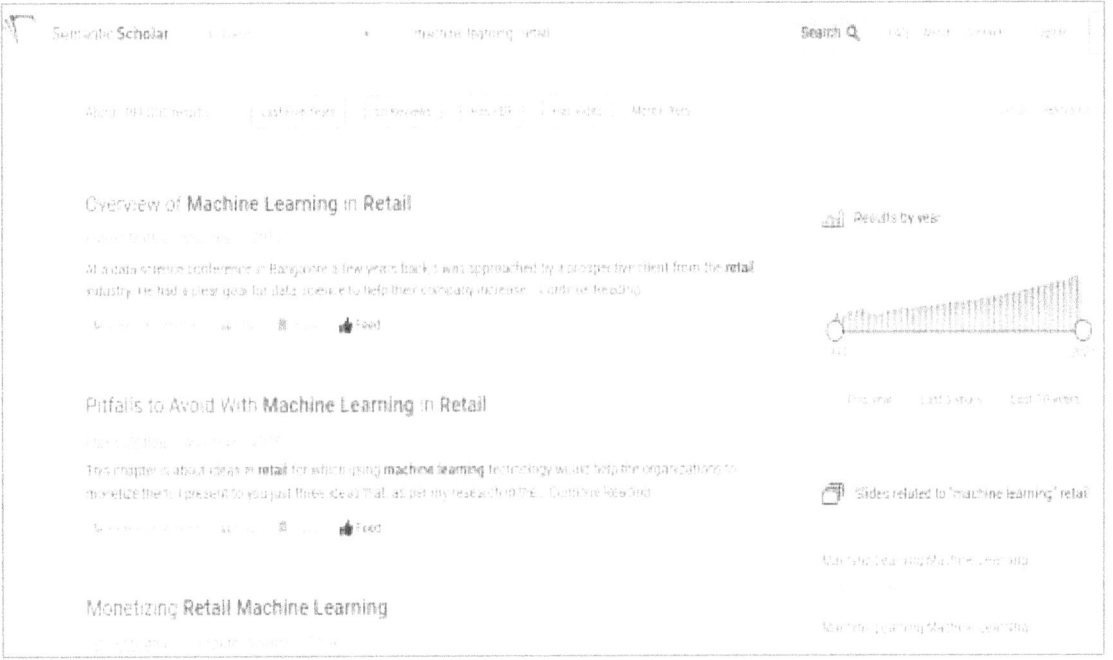

7.5.4 Researchgate

Researchgate is another research publication search engine that covers the following topics:

- Engineering
- Computer Science
- Medicine
- Biology
- Physics
- Mathematics
- Chemistry

An example X-ray search is as illustrated below:

site:researchgate.net "machine learning" retail

site:researchgate.net "machine learning" retail ("yahoo.ca" OR "yahoo.de" OR "gmail.com" OR "outlook.com")

7.6 Startups

Startups give a view of the emerging competitors that could disrupt your business models and may rewrite the rules of the game. Following are some of the available tools that you could deploy to develop competitive intelligence reports.

Owler.com - You can create company lists and receive news about these specific companies through the web or email

Pitchbook.com – You can obtain information related to employee count, office locations, contact information, financing history, financials, top executive names and board members

An example X-ray of Pitchbook looking for funding info on companies based out of NY with an employee size of around 1700 is illustrated below:

site:pitchbook.com funding computer software new york employees 1700

Following are some of the Startup sites that you can explore for research:

https://bangalore.startups-list.com/

http://10000startups.com/our-startups

https://headstart.in/chapter/bangalore

https://www.f6s.com/

https://eazyhire.in/

https://www.startupers.com/

https://www.ventureloop.com

Top 100 European Startups

Figure 45:

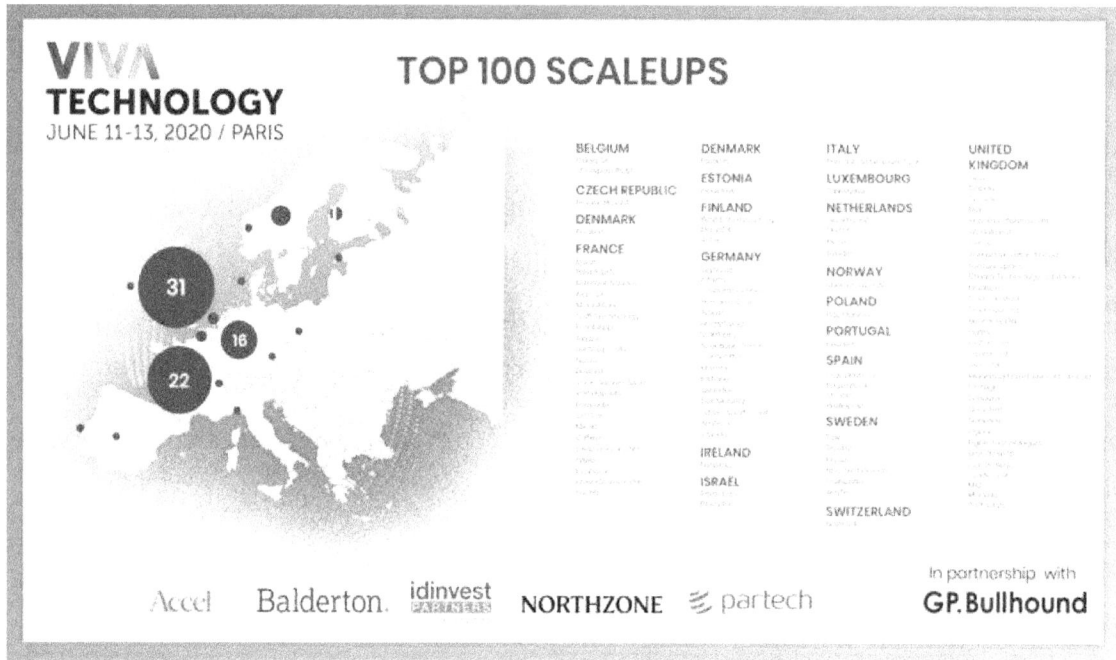

7.7 Budget Knowledge

If your focus is on Government bids in US and Canada, their budget documents list the upcoming projects, the budget estimate, and if you are lucky, 3, 5 or 10 year plans are also published on the city or country or state or township website portals.

It's a valuable source of information that you can utilize to plan for your account managers to position your firm and the product/service and for pricing the bid effectively.

Example of City of Toronto IT 2020 Budget document:

https://www.toronto.ca/legdocs/mmis/2020/bu/bgrd/backgroundfile-141430.pdf

Example of City of Chicago 2020 Budget documents:

https://www.chicago.gov/city/en/depts/obm/supp_info/budgetdocuments.html

Example of King County, Washington state budget related info:

https://kingcounty.gov/depts/executive/performance-strategy-budget/budget/2019-2020-Proposed-Budget.aspx

7.8 Alerts

Google alerts is an excellent avenue to monitor what your competitors are doing.

All one has to do is type in a company name or any topic of interest and enter the email address of where the alert should be sent to. There are several options like Language, frequency, type of alerts (blog, news etc.)

Figure 46: Google Alerts

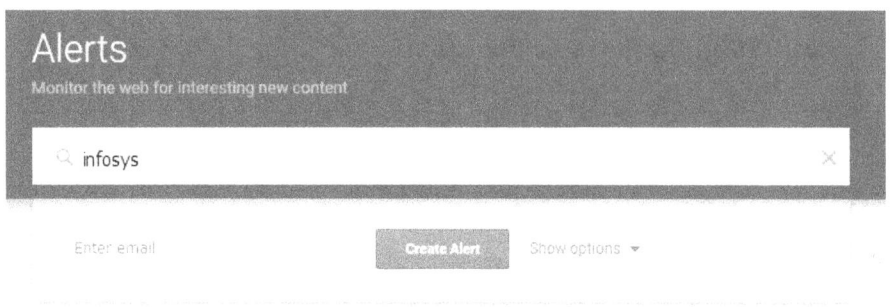

Figure 47: Google Alerts options

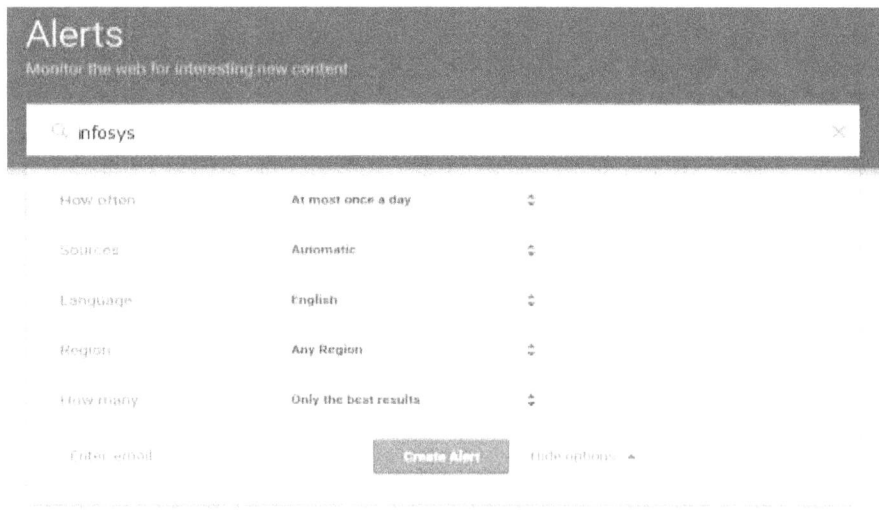

An alternative to Google alerts is Talkwalker. It allows you to setup alerts with filters for news, blogs, Twitter, discussion forums only tracking in 22 different languages and you can narrow it down to source country as well. The familiar Boolean operators work including wildcard.

You can compare two different companies here and see the top themes etc. and you can also see the influencers for a specific search query you may have.

7.9 Competitor websites

While reviewing a competitor or an existing/future client prospect, the first place one would need to review is their website.

Such websites are a goldmine to understand their operations, priorities, growth avenues, growth levers, acquisitions, awards, financial updates, partnerships, expansion strategies and product or service portfolio changes.

Product page review

A detailed review of the product pages on your competitors' websites, that includes product descriptions, product reviews by customers, support articles, forums and product info graphics, can reveal how a competitor is explaining their products and communicating the benefits of it.

Identify any information that maybe missing, why it is not present and utilize the weaknesses to better position your product against them.

Example: RFPAutomationFactory (A fictitious Proposal automation Software Company)

It is in the company's best interest not to refer to features that are weak or not fully developed as they wish to put their best foot forward.

When automation is in a conversation, invariably AI/ML is talked about very frequently. Analyze whether they do refer to it and if so, to what level, and in what context.

Analyze the product UX (thru product demos) and see if there are usability issues.

Analyze the product support pages to see if there are any gaps that your company can focus on while competing against them.

Review the testimonials to see if their customers talk about product features that are missing in the product descriptions.

Third party review sites

Third party review sites like Capterra Softwareadvice FeaturedCustomers G2 FinancesOnline TechnologyEvaluations IT Central Station may provide an overview of the product's recent experiences, any grievances, and recommendations. Any reviews more than 2 years old can be discounted.

Competitors do not just sit quiet. They will be monitoring you as well to see if there any gaps or strengths that they do not have and eagerly working to bridge it. Review your competitors regularly so that your decisions and pitch books to clients can be tweaked.

Marketing messaging

Every company will be promoting their product or service for prospects. They will feature testimonials, case studies, YouTube channel and Instagram video as part of the marketing messages. By tracking such information, you will get to know of their key clients, how they are winning them and their method of building their brand strength.

You may also track their Press releases, event attendance (the events they are skipping is also a good data point to track) and event sponsorships to get a better understanding of how they are promoting their brand.

Pay attention to what content of theirs gets the most engagement on social media.

Tracking Key employees

Also, review the profiles of your competitor's key employees on Linkedin and other media in terms of their background i.e. qualifications, skills, certifications, previous jobs, current role and responsibilities etc.

Closely track key sales personnel hiring and off boarding. It could be a sign of booming time ahead or a retention problem or sales not going in the right direction.

Investor Relations

If it's a public listed company, also check the "**Investor relations**" section of the website. You will find their quarterly, annual financial statements, analyst briefings along with corporate governance, and Social responsibility statements in some cases.

Their quarterly and annual reports give precise information about the risks, revenue, margins, C&B of the management, financial health, subsidiaries, partnerships etc.

Career section

Scraping their career section job postings can provide an advanced view of the current and future projects, technology investment areas, functional investment areas, skills they are looking to hire for, new location manufacturing or service delivery centre intelligence among others.

Office locations

Office location additions are a good signal of a company's focus areas of growth. Many a time, this silent addition of office could come about before an announcement of hiring plans, funding or product-service-support initiatives tied to the new location.

Executive moves and updates

As referred to in Section **7.1** where you can x-ray a website to track executive moves, an addition or a removal of an executive can signal quite a bit. It is important to discuss what this entails and share the learning's with the impacted teams.

For example, if the VP, Product is removed, it could mean there may have been challenges with the speed of product innovation or the features being implemented have not caught the imagination of customers or there maybe reliability issues at play. This insight could be a good input for the sales team's competitive positioning or marketing team's competitive campaigns.

Talent Intelligence

Some companies like Philips, Intel, SAP, Google, Facebook, Microsoft, Verizon, Amazon, J&J, Accenture, RBS, G-Research, standard industries, Qualcomm, IBM, Redbull, Stryker, Nike, Lowes, Wells Fargo, Mastercard, United Health Group, Sony Pictures Entertainment, Deloitte already have an in-house talent intelligence team that provide location suitability, talent availability studies to the Talent Acquisition and upper management.

Employee Reviews

Employer rating websites provide a platform for employees to rate their employers in terms of work culture, structured processes for interviewing, salary levels, benefits, grievances, the things that may or may not be working well. The reviews may serve as a data point to understand some of the inner workings of the company.

An example of secondary source CI information dissemination

Recruiting and employer brand perspective (Quarter ending)

Category	Firm 1	Firm 2
Jobs	150 new jobs posting. Key roles they are investing in: RPA Practice Lead for Europe RPA Auditor Salesforce CRM Practice Head Cyber security chief for UK VP, Marketing – France	125 new job postings Key roles they are investing in: UIPath Practice Head Enterprise Healthcare architect for entire Americas Global Talent Intelligence Head VP, M&A - Canada
Leadership change	Current Global pursuit lead is leaving.	Global CTO has left
Key sales reps	Pursuit lead for EMEA opening	Sales head for Americas opening
Geography Expansion or contraction	Opening an office in Cologne, Germany, quite a few roles advertised for the startup operations Doubling up their offices in California	Opening an office in Norway to take care of Scandinavian market, so few roles advertised there Opening a delivery services office in India to increase their capabilities
Employer ratings	Glassdoor rating improved from 3.5 to 3.9	Glassdoor rating improved from 3.9 to 4.0
Awards And Recognition	Received Best place to work award They are now in the Forbes – Best Employers for Diversity list	They are now in the Working Mother: Top 100 Companies List

Example of Marketing CI information dissemination

Category	Firm 1	Firm 2
Content management	SharePoint is now their CMS	OpenText is now their CMS
Social media	They are actively promoting articles on dev.to, Dzone. Their website also has a lot of product blogs especially along the lines of AML solutions,	They have created a lot of YouTube videos around Remote working solutions and it is paying off with a lot of publicly announced customer wins.
Product and support Reviews	There have been quite a few positive product reviews of their RPA solution on Capterra, IT Central Station.	Their AML product support has taken a beating with quite a few customers complaining about it on their product support portals and Twitter.
Public Relations	Their new product vision and forthcoming releases and upgrades have been extensively covered in eweek, CIO and other tech publications.	They have chaired 10 webinars around the topics of AI, Future of work, RPA, Reskilling workforce, Fintech.
Events	They are exhibiting at Women in Big Data, Microsoft Ignite, Deep Learning Summit	They are exhibiting at STEP, Gartner Data and Analytics Summit, RSA Conference.
Major sponsorships	They are now the official partners for LPGA Golf	They are the Corporate partner for "Girls who code".

HR perspective (Quarter ending)

Category	Firm 1	Firm 2
Jobs	150 new jobs posting. Key roles they are investing in: D&I Lead for Americas Salesforce CRM Practice Head Cyber security chief for UK VP, Marketing – France	125 new job postings Key roles they are investing in: UIPath Practice Head Global Talent Intelligence Head VP, M&A - Canada
Leadership change	Current Global HR lead is leaving.	Global CHRO has left
Metrics	<ul><li>Revenue / Employee</li><li>Net income / Employee</li><li>Cost Per Hire Versus SHRM (US Only) benchmark (Up or Down)</li><li>Cost of Vacancy</li></ul>	<ul><li>Revenue / Employee</li><li>Net income / Employee</li><li>Cost Per Hire Versus SHRM (US Only) benchmark (Up or Down)</li><li>Cost of Vacancy</li></ul>
Sourcing Channels usage	Linkedin – Extensive usage and jobs posted regularly Twitter – Jobs or new Talent additions (for sales, product marketing) Instagram – For Employer branding and talent magnet Job Boards (specifics) – Naukri, CareerBuilder	Linkedin – Extensive usage and jobs posted regularly Twitter – Jobs or new Talent additions (for sales, product marketing) Job Boards (specifics) – Indeed, CareerBuilder, Dice.com, Crunchboard.com
Geography Expansion or contraction	Opening an office in Cologne, Germany, quite a few roles advertised for the startup operations Doubling up their offices in California	Opening an office in Norway to take care of Scandinavian market, so few roles advertised there Opening a delivery services office in India to increase their capabilities
Employer ratings	Glassdoor rating improved from 3.5 to 3.9	Glassdoor rating improved from 3.9 to 4.0
Awards And Recognition	Received Best place to work award They are now in the Forbes – Best Employers for Diversity list	They are now in the Working Mother: Top 100 Companies List

Likewise, you may want to create similar set of reports for Product and service lines, sales, Finance and other areas to provide a complete picture of the competitor moves.

Case study

Assume you are working for a Fintech firm providing insurance solutions to the Public on only Mobile devices, what are the things you would look for as part of competitive study?

7.10 Competitor analysis tools

Following are some of the tools that can be used to review competitor or client websites:

7.10.1 SimilarWeb

If you are looking to review website statistics in terms of the traffic sources, traffic by countries, keywords used, pages per visit, average visit duration, which social media is driving traffic, you can utilize SimilarWeb for this purpose.

You can compare one competitor against you or one other competitor as well. The "free" version gives a good source of information.

Example Analysis of Wipro website:

Figure 48: SimilarWeb

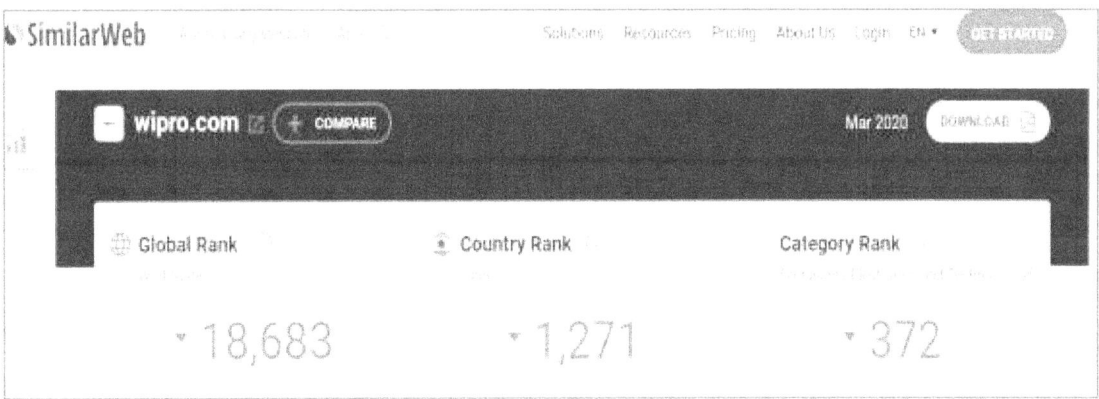

Figure 49: SimilarWeb Traffic Overview

Figure 50: SimilarWeb Traffic by Countries

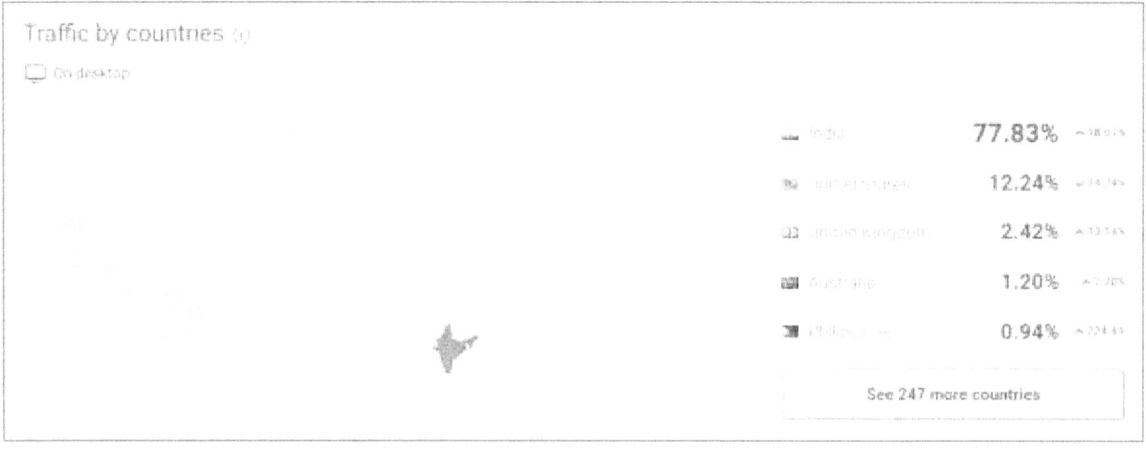

Figure 51: SimilarWeb Traffic by sources

Figure 52: SimilarWeb Audience Interests

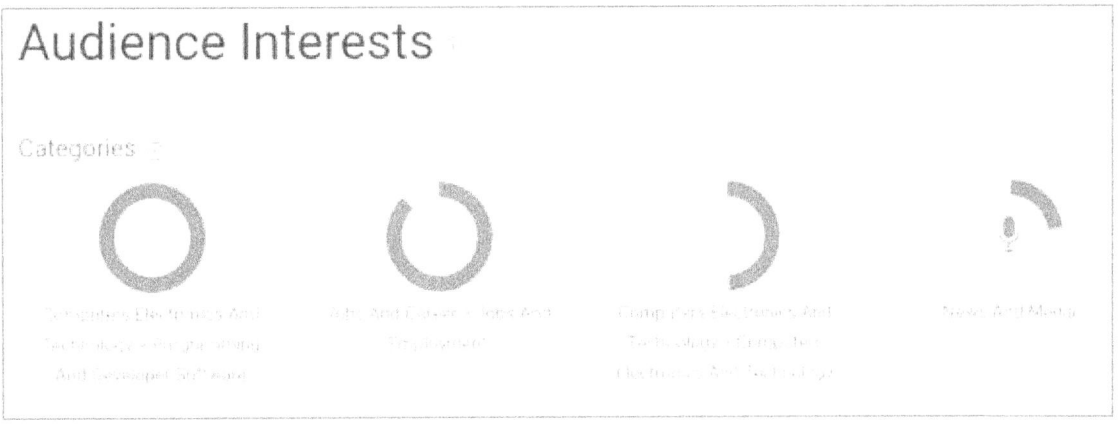

7.10.2 Mediatoolkit

This tool can monitor online mentions of your brand in real-time, and will let you know about every article, hash tag or comment mentioning your business. You also can compare with competitors, track current industry topics, find social media influencers, identify engaging posts and analyze brand sentiment.

7.10.3 VisualPing

You can monitor a webpage when it changes thru an email alert. You can drag the cursor to the section of the page or a full to see if any changes have come about. Pretty nifty indeed.

Figure 53: VisualPing of Accenture.com/jobs webpage change tracking

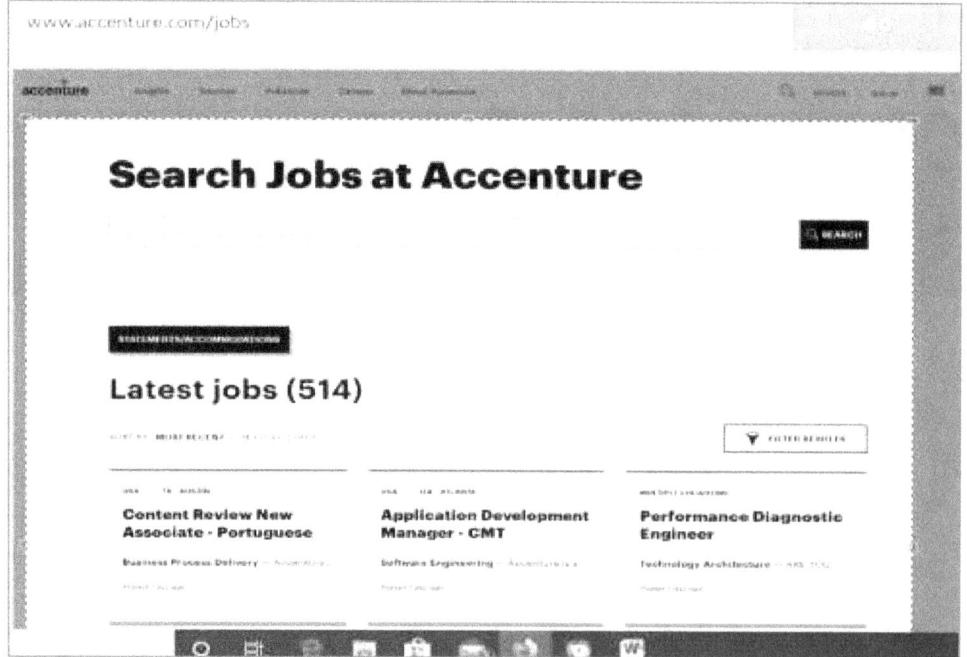

7.10.4 Feedly

Feedly – Excellent tool to keep up with the topics and trends you care about. It's AI assistant Leo, helps you to filter out the noise.

Figure 54: Feedly

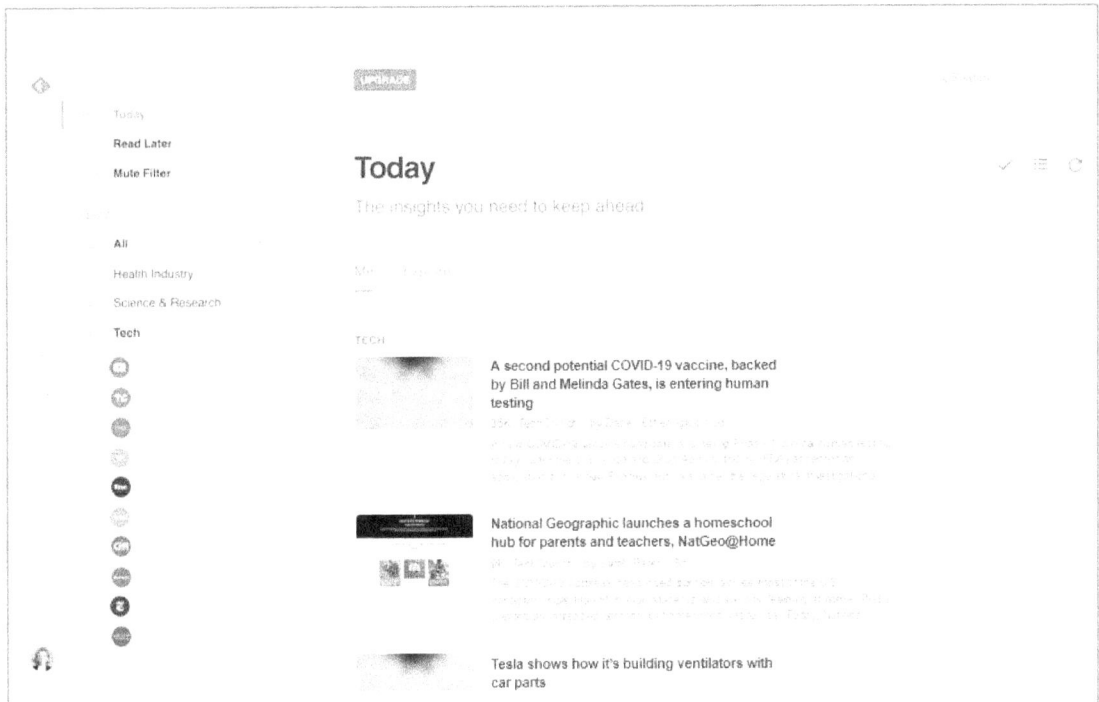

7.10.5 Datanyze

Another tool that you can utilize is Datanyze which allows you to upload 50 customer websites at a time and receive a free technological profile of them via email.

7.10.6 RivalIQ

Using this tool, you can measure your firm's Twitter, Instagram and Facebook snapshot against your rivals

Figure 55: RivalIQ

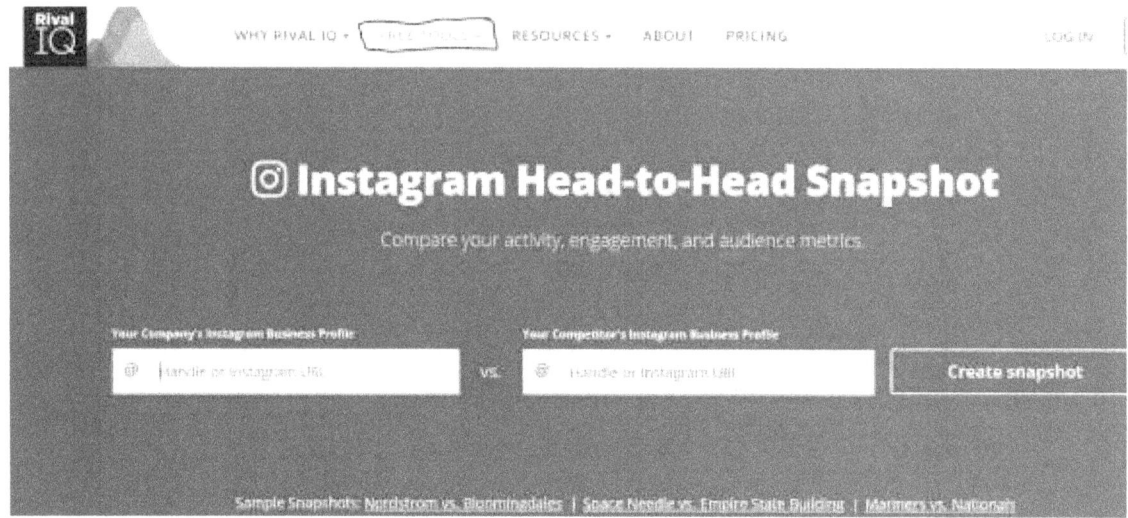

7.10.7 Craft

Craft is an interesting tool to track the past, present and future of companies

Figure 56: Netflix review

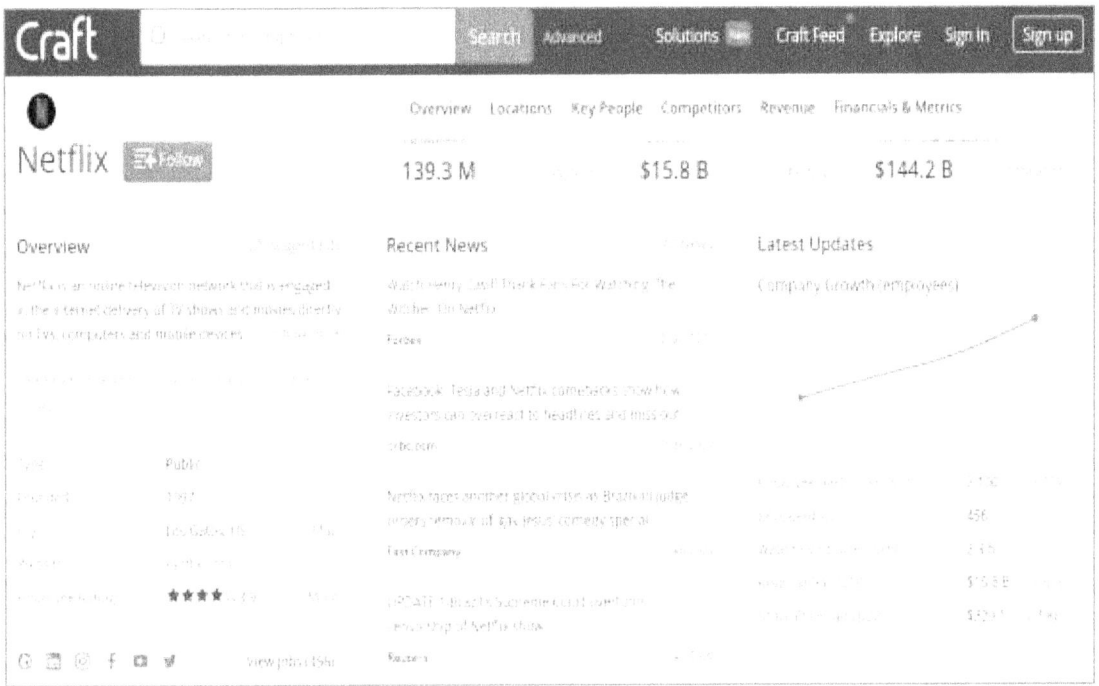

7.10.8 Whatruns

You need to install **Whatruns** plugin on your browser.

An example illustration of finding out what is running on the TCS website is as below. If are into digital marketing or marketing automation or advertising software provision and you wish to know who is using which software, this information can be very valuable to your sales team.

Figure 57: Whatruns

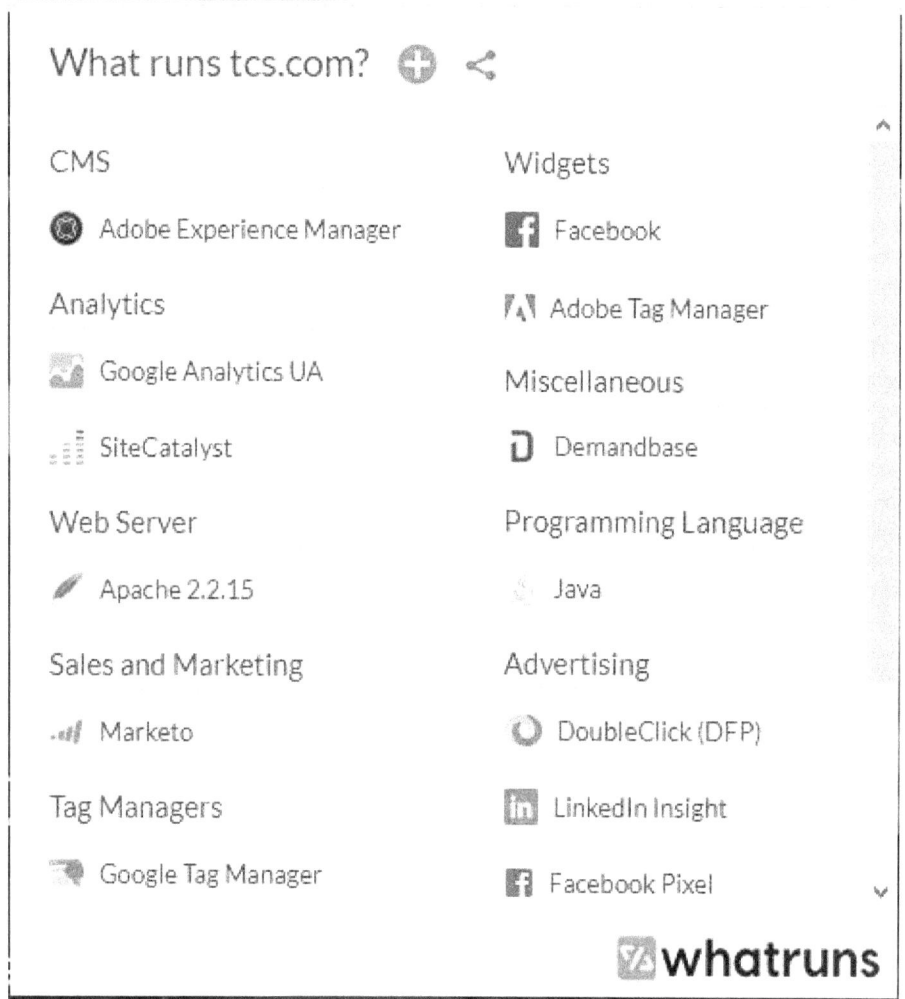

7.10.9 Builtwith

Builtwith is an excellent tool to find the technology changes on a competitor website in terms of the framework used, widgets, CMS used, email and web hosting providers, advertising networks, languages supported.

Bulitwith scans websites and also provides lead generation, competitive analysis and business intelligence tool providing technology adoption, ecommerce data and usage analytics for the internet.

If you are a B2B software provider, and you wanted to target competitor's customers, you would first need a list of the clients. Builtwith can provide the list upon demand for a price.

Figure 58: Builtwith

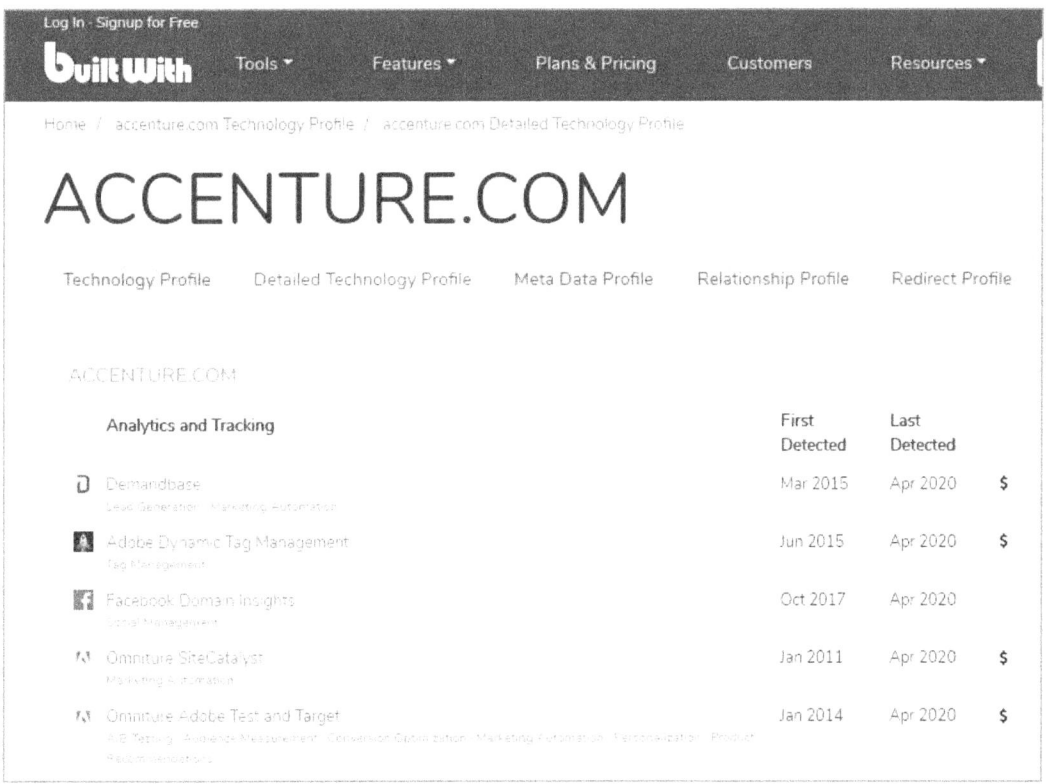

7.11 Trends

Following are some of the websites, blogs to research the latest trends in the marketplace.

Tech magazines

https://www.eweek.com

Information Security magazines

https://www.infosecurity-magazine.com

https://www.scmagazineuk.com/

https://onlinedegrees.sandiego.edu/top-cyber-security-blogs-websites/

https://www.securityweek.com/

Business Magazines

- Harvard Business Review
- Forbes
- CIOReview
- CIOReviewIndia

CIOReview has a Twitter handle **@cioreview** that you can utilize to review some updates.

Analytics India Magazine highlights the Data science, AI, Big data innovations, players, and challenges shaping the future of India through promotion and discussion of thoughts by individuals who want to change the world.

For the last 2 years, they are showcasing the best data science firms to work for and this year's list is shown below:

https://analyticsindiamag.com/11-best-firms-in-india-for-data-scientists-to-work-for-2020/

7.12 Research firms

Some of the prominent Research agencies that you might want to follow is as follows:

- Gartner
- Forrester
- HFS Research
- Everest Group
- IDC
- IHS Markit
- Omdia

You can review their magic quadrants, Top 10 lists, analyst reports, competitor analysis report (subscription basis) and get a good understanding of where your competitors are and where the market is headed.

All the research agencies have their Twitter handle and you can follow the individual analysts affiliated with them or the company itself.

7.13 Associations

There is an organization called "Strategic and Competitive Intelligence professionals" which awards certification for various disciplines within CI. It has 17 chapters in US and 22 other chapters worldwide (Bangalore and Mumbai in India).

The organization provides online training programmers and they also organize an annual "Intellicon" conference in US and Europe.

They have a twitter handle **@scip** that you can follow for updates and you can check the "followers" for it.

7.14 Companies specializing in CI

Following are some of the companies specializing in CI.

- CompetellQ
- Digimind
- Fletcher/CSI
- Crayon
- Comintelli
- ValueNotes (Based out of Pune)

7.15 Organization charts

Organization charts are pure gold from a competitive research perspective. It depicts a reporting or relationship hierarchy and structure and gives a good understanding of how decisions are made and the internal dynamics.

From a recruiting perspective, it is quite labour intensive to develop the entire organization charts of your competitors but it could be worth it in the end.

7.15.1 theOrg.com

https://theorg.com is a neat little organization mapping website and very simple to use.

Example search of Microsoft

C-suite names, EVPs are listed along with the Board of Director names. Upon Clicking the CEO name, you get a list of direct reports.

Figure 59: Microsoft executive level Org Chart

Figure 60: Microsoft Board and Advisors

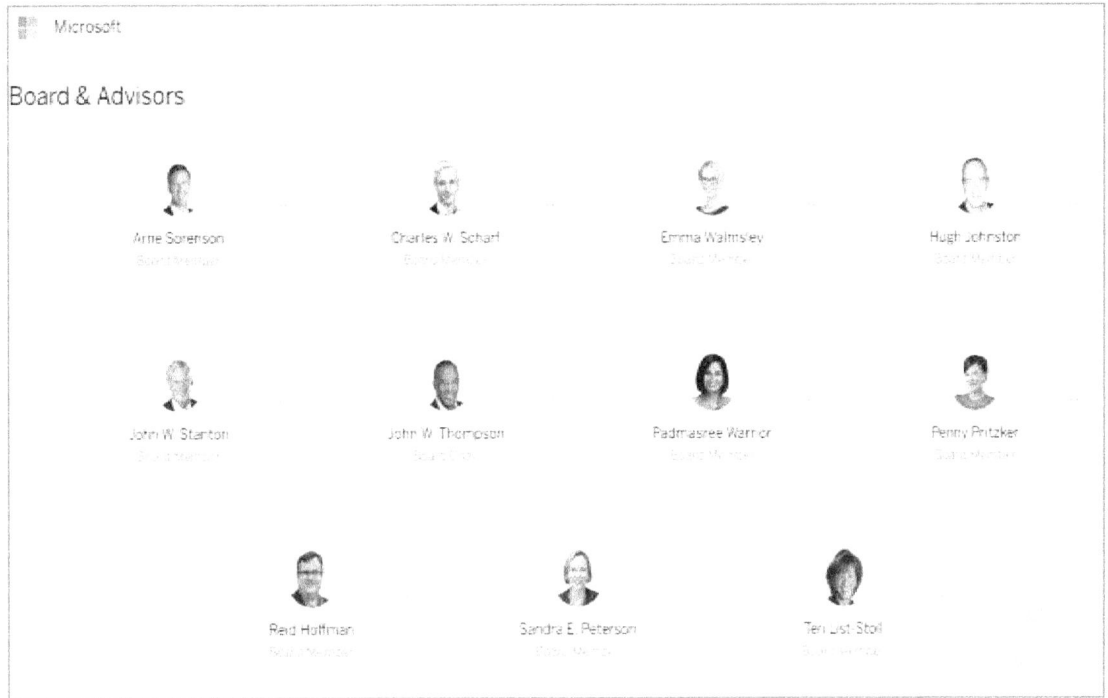

7.15.2 Scout by LeadIQ

Scout by LeadIQ is a free chrome extension to do organization mapping

Install Chrome browser, and then go to chrome web store and look for "LeadIQ" chrome extension.

Once installed, it will display an icon (dog) in the chrome browser on the top right hand side of the screen.

Click the icon, it will ask you to input your name, email address, company name and login.

Upon login, you can search by company name and it will list the companies (some have many subsidiaries as well).

Navigate to a specific name and you obtain a list of some of the top employees involved at the firm. A click of a name reveals the email address, so there is no more guessing of the email pattern.

Figure 61: LeadIQ in the Google Chrome store

Example search of Walmart VP, analytics below:

Figure 62: LeadIQ results

Chapter 8 Other Search Avenues

8.1 Conference websites

Another tool you could potentially use is x-raying event management websites to obtain conference and events listing in your location or nearby locations. Sometimes these events may even have public attendee lists but at the very least they will turn up speaker bios.

Examples of a targeted search of conferences are illustrated below:

site:eventbrite.com (bangalore | bengaluru) (tech OR design OR product OR software OR code)

site:townscript.com (bangalore | bengaluru) (tech OR design OR product OR software OR code)

site:sched.com (bangalore | bengaluru) marketing

To find attendee lists targeting the first and last names (Google search)

ext:pdf (inurl:conclave OR inurl:roundtable OR inurl:conference OR inurl:seminar OR inurl:event OR inurl:webinar OR inurl:meetup OR inurl:workshop OR inurl:Expo) "first name" "last name" technology -form -register –sponsorship

ext:pdf inurl:(conclave OR roundtable OR conference OR seminar OR event OR webinar OR meetup OR workshop OR Expo) "first name" "last name" technology -form -register -sponsorship

Likewise replace ext:pdf with ext:xls or ext:xlsx or ext:doc or ext:docx to obtain different results

To find attendee lists in the insurance sector (Google search)

filetype:pdf inurl:(conclave OR roundtable OR conference OR seminar OR event OR webinar OR meetup OR workshop OR Expo) (directory OR roster OR attendees OR delegates OR membership OR participants) insurance -sponsorship -form -application

8.2 File sharing sites

You can use the file sharing sites to search any documents/presentations uploaded by companies based on a specific topic.

Example search string is:

site:slideshare.net "digital transformation" Accenture

Following are some example search string that could be used on AWS, Google, Scribd:

inurl:amazonaws.com (engineer|developer|specialist) intitle:resume OR inurl:resume -sample -career –tips

site:google.com inurl:sites OR inurl:drive OR inurl:docs "resume" backend developer "boston" -sample

site:docs.google.com/spreadsheets "staff directory -example

site:docs.google.com/document developer bangalore intitle:(CV OR resume OR vitae) -example -sample -template -jobs -free

site:scribd.com resume "ecommerce" manager seattle WA

8.3 Image search

You can run a diversity based search in Google which you can accomplish by typing the search term in the search bar and click **"Images"** tab to see the results.

Notice the usage of **(She OR her OR hers OR woman OR women)** to obtain gender specific results.

Example Boolean string to use is: ("chief digital officer") (She OR her OR hers OR woman OR women)

Figure 63: Google Image search

Chapter 9 Federal bids

Introduction

You may regularly bid for US, Canadian, UK, Australian or European Public sector procurements. The difficulty in fulfilling the obligations of a contracting win lies solely on the access and hiring security clearance professionals. Although different levels of clearances exist, these individuals are not that easily visible from a social media perspective, so an old school method of relationship building and trust has to be formed.

The security clearance is required if you have an offer to work for a Government agency on a full time basis or on contract with a consulting vendor who works for the Government, primarily to have handling and access privileges.

NATO Clearance

NATO works with sensitive information and limits access to individuals with proper security clearances. Unintended or malicious disclosure could cause damage to NATO's forces, its members or its mission. Therefore, classified information is protected through a series of security procedures based on its markings.

NATO with its 29 member countries has 4 levels of security classification:

- NATO RESTRICTED
- NATO CONFIDENTIAL
- NATO SECRET
- COSMIC TOP SECRET

9.1 US perspective

All federal agencies require security clearance but there are varying levels depending on the access privileges. The primary requirement is for the individual to be an US citizen.

There are 3 levels of clearance:

- Confidential – Unauthorized Disclosure by which some damage occurs to the national security
- Secret - Unauthorized Disclosure by which serious damage occurs to the national security
- Top secret - Unauthorized Disclosure by which grave damage occurs to the national security

Clearance	Screening activities	Processing times
Confidential	Verification of identity and background Verification of educational and professional credentials Personal and professional references check Credit check Criminal record check Fingerprinting Public records check	Up to 3 months
Secret	Same as above with possible neighbour check-ins, co-worker interviews, scrutiny of tax returns, drug, alcohol and sexual status	6-12 months
Top Secret	Above, and additionally Polygraph tests, personal interview, medical exam, Psychological evaluation	>1 year

All these clearances are re-investigated every 5 years

Some classified information is extremely sensitive that the extra protection measures applied to Top Secret information is not sufficient. Such information is Sensitive Compartmented Information (SCI), which includes intelligence sources, methods, and processes, and Special Access Programs (SAPs), which are highly sensitive projects and programs.

DoD operates a security program different from other agencies. Even if one were to possess a secret/top secret clearance from another agency, it may not get transferred. They generate around 80% of all clearances.

Department of Energy has 2 levels of clearance, Q and L (Similar to Secret and Top Secret)

When a security clearance expires i.e. (when someone leaves the military or leaves the government civilian job or contractor job), it can be reactivated within 24 months, as long as it falls within the re-evaluation period. Hence the race to source and hire active clearance holders and there are huge rewards and bonus payouts for sourcing such individuals.

Clearance personnel numbers

According to the Office of Director of National Intelligence, as of 1st October 2017, there were 4,030,625 individuals found eligible to hold a clearance (Top Secret clearance numbers are 1,309,793)

Sourcing Cleared personnel

So, now you understand the value of individuals holding these security clearances. Next, the question is how to find them? Below, please find areas across the internet where you can search for clearance jobs, talent, and how to source for them.

Clearance job sites

https://clearedjobs.net/

https://www.clearancejobs.com

https://cybersecjobs.com/

https://www.defensetalent.com

https://clearedconnections.com

Discussion forums

https://discuss.clearancejobsblog.com/

https://forum.federalsoup.com/default.aspx?g=topics&f=22

https://www.reddit.com/r/SecurityClearance/comments/b1387c/rru_scattered_castles_into_jpas/

Where can I find lists of US government contractors?

One avenue is look at the Top 100 US Government contractors report from "Federal Procurement Data system" and can search based on the companies to find relevant clearance personnel working at other companies

Additional source is Washington Technology, which lists Top 100 Prime contractors in the areas of IT, professional services, telecommunications and other high-tech services areas

Another additional source is Bloomberg Government Top 200 Federal contractor's reports.

Other option is to look up GSA schedules in Google, which companies often showcase on their website, to identify competitors not found in the Top lists above.

An example Google search would be "GSA schedule" federal government -what -how –advantage

Linkedin search

Typical searches in Linkedin will give some results but very little of Top secret personnel who are the hardest to find and hire.

Some clearance specific key word searches you can utilize are:

Security clearance OR "Public Trust clearance" OR Secret OR "DoD Secret" OR "Top Secret" OR "Top Secret Clearance" OR "TS SCI" OR "TS-SCI" OR "TS/SCI" OR "Special Access Program" OR "TS/SCI w/ Full Scope" OR "Full Scope Poly" OR "TS/SCI w/FSP OR "FS-Polygraph" OR "Special Agent" OR SIDA OR "Sensitive Compartmented Information" OR SCI OR "Counter Intelligence poly" OR "CI Poly" OR "Lifestyle poly" OR "TS/SBI" OR "TS/SSBI"

Even a full scope Polygraph from some agency say from NSA may not be equivalent with say DHS Full Scope Polygraph.

JPAS or Scattered Castles (for intelligence agencies) is the only place to check an individual's current clearance status.

US Navy or Airforce contractor personnel typically have a requirement of travelling.

A search term of CONUS (Lower 48 states) or OCONUS (Outside of Continental United States) would be handy as well.

An indirect way of finding cleared individuals is by utilizing specific department names such as:

- Federal Bureau of Investigation (FBI)
- Department of Defense (DoD)
- Defense intelligence Agency (DIA)
- NSA
- NGIA
- Department of Homeland Security (DHS)
- Department of State – Bureau of Intelligence and Research
- NASA
- CIA
- National Reconnaissance Office
- Air Force Intelligence- Surveillance and Reconnaissance
- Army Military Intelligence
- Office of Naval Intelligence
- Marine Corps Intelligence
- Pentagon

Federal procurement registry search

One source you can check is the past program names (examples being F35 or F22 or F18A) in the RFP/RFQ solicitations in Federal Government procurement sites.

Often you see the company names being listed as the current incumbent vendors (Prime and sub-contractors) in the solicitations and typically these are listed 6-12 months before the actual contract expiry. One can utilize this information and cross-reference it with other sources to identify personnel working on such programs.

Some maybe brand new programs that you can add to your database search list for future usage.

Some of these registries are:

https://beta.sam.gov/ - All Fed Biz opportunities

https://procurement.jsc.nasa.gov/busops.asp - NASA Johnson Space Centre

https://www.dibbs.bsm.dla.mil - Defense Logistics Agency

Typical Job Titles at Federal Government Agencies

- Thermal engineers
- Mechanical Engineers
- Identity and Directory Management Lead
- Program Analyst
- Help desk or service desk agents
- Software engineer
- RF Engineer
- Electrical engineer
- Program and Project Managers
- System Integrator
- Systems Administrator
- Stress and Structural Engineer
- Systems and Network Engineers
- Software Programmers
- Intelligence Analyst
- Hardware Engineers
- Application Developers
- Data Methodologists
- Strategy and change management consultant
- Facilities consultant
- Testing Engineers
- Contracts Management Professionals
- Aerospace and Aero structure Engineers
- SATCOM network support analysts
- Cyber security analysts and managers
- Logistics support associates and analyst

Areas where Government Agencies hire contractors for

- Systems Integration
- Network support
- Missile Defense and security Systems (warning, environment monitoring)
- SATCOM
- Space Systems and Exploration
- Intelligence, Surveillance, and Reconnaissance Platforms
- Cyber security Analysis
- Radar and Air Defense Systems
- Logistical Support
- Drones
- Secure Unified Communications
- Combat and Fire Control Systems
- Port Harbour and Perimeter Defense

Scrape contractor Job postings

You can scrape every job posted by the Fed contractors and can pick up a lot of specific system names unique to that Government agency, which can you utilize for future use. To Illustrate, an example of a SAIC job posting with system highlighters as below:

Figure 92: Job Ad highlighting for system keywords

Scanning the ATS

It would be worthwhile to scan the ATS to pick the existing resumes of clearance holders, and scrape specific systems keywords while being in the employ of the Federal Government, just like the above option and build your search strings.

Facebook search

Some enlisted personnel are on warships and they typically have USS or USNS as a starting point. https://www.militaryfactory.com/modern-navy/united-states-navy.asp has a good list of the current fleet by name.

Look up the fleet by name, and where its base station is in US and search from there.

An example search could be:

site:facebook.com "profile photo" "USS Carl Vinson" "san diego" engineer

Enlisted personnel cannot be hired due to the contract agreements (4 or 8 years or up to 20 years) but they would potentially know folks who maybe leaving the service after their service timeline expiry or know people in other service areas with relevant clearances.

9.2 Canadian perspective

There are 3 levels of clearance:

- Enhanced Reliability (Level I)– Unauthorized Disclosure by which some damage occurs to the national security
- Secret (Level II) - Unauthorized Disclosure by which serious damage occurs to the national security.
- Top Secret (Level III) - Unauthorized Disclosure by which grave damage occurs to the national security.

Clearance	Screening activities	Background check	Validity (Years)
Enhanced Reliability	Verification of identity and background Verification of educational and professional credentials Personal and professional references check (personal refs may not be checked by every agency) Credit and financial check (may differ from agency to agency) Criminal record check Fingerprinting	5 years	10
Secret	Above and additionally CSIS assessment	10	10
Top Secret	Above, and additionally Polygraph tests, personal interview, neighbour checkins	10	5

Contract award notices search

Government of Canada discloses all awarded contracts under $10k and over $10k and it is searchable by year, company, country origin, agreement type, contract values spread across goods, services and construction, along with departmental wise of contracts and values awarded. The data is also available for download and can be found here:

(https://open.canada.ca/en/search/contracts?f%5B0%5D=contracts_country_of_origin_en%3ACanada

9.3 UK perspective

UK has 4 categories of security levels as described below:

Baseline: This is an entry level Pre-employment check to provide an appropriate level of assurance as to the trustworthiness, integrity, and probable reliability of prospective employees. It has two types Baseline Personnel Security Standard (BPSS) and Enhanced Baseline Standard (EBS).

Counter Terrorist Check (CTC): This is undertaken if an individual is working in proximity to public figures, or requires unescorted access to certain military, civil, industrial or commercial establishments assessed to be at particular risk from terrorist attack.

Security Check (SC): This is undertaken to determine a person's character and personal circumstances such that they can be trusted to work in a position that involves long-term, frequent and uncontrolled access to SECRET assets. Also has an enhanced Security check type (eSC)

Developed Vetting: (DV) in addition to SC, this detailed investigation is required when an individual has long term, frequent and uncontrolled access to 'Top Secret' information. This is re-investigated after 5 years and every 7 years if there is a continuing need, depending on circumstances. Also has an enhanced Developed Vetting (eDV) type.

Clearance	Screening activities	Residential requirement	Validity (Years)
Counter Terrorist Check	<ul><li>Baseline Personnel Security Standard (BPSS)</li><li>Departmental / Company Records Check</li><li>Security Questionnaire</li><li>Criminal Record Check</li><li>Security Service Check</li><li>Interview maybe required</li></ul>	3 years in UK	3
Security check	Same as above but with a credit reference check. This is transferrable between government departments. It is reviewed every 10 years.	5 years in UK	5 for contractors and 10 for FTEs
Developed Vetting (DV)	Same as above with additional requirements of:<ul><li>DV Security Questionnaire</li><li>Credit Reference Check and review of personal finances</li><li>Check of medical and psychological information provided</li><li>Personal Interview of applicant</li><li>Interviews with character referees and current and previous supervisors.</li></ul>Change of circumstances (divorce, new partner etc.) has to be disclosed even after getting the clearance	10 Years in UK	Depends on the nature of the project. Re-check after 5 years.

Sourcing Cleared personnel

SecuritaclearedJobs is the largest UK Job board for cleared personnel.

Linkedin search

Typical searches in Linkedin will give some results but very little of DV personnel who are the hardest to find and hire.

Some clearance specific key word searches you can utilize are:

"Security clearance" OR "Military clearance" OR "military cleared" OR "security cleared" OR "DV" OR BPSS OR EBS OR eDV OR SC OR CTC

Where can I find lists of UK government contractors?

Many of such lists can be obtained thru RTI Act. Some sources are below:

https://www.statista.com/statistics/603376/uk-mod-percentage-of-expenditure-to-top-suppliers/

https://www.gov.uk/government/organisations/ministry-of-defence/about/procurement#our-supply-base

https://www.gov.uk/contracts-finder

Where can I find contracts to bid?

MoD Defense contracts (https://www.defenceonline.co.uk/stakeholders/mod-defence-contracts-online/)

https://www.crowncommercial.gov.uk

TED (https://ted.europa.eu/TED/browse/browseByBO.do)

This gives an opportunity to review the program names, systems involved that you can utilize for your future searches

9.4 Australian perspective

Australia has 4 levels of clearance.

Clearance	Screening activities	Background check
Baseline	Lowest level check and involves vetting of: - Personal details - Overseas travel - Employment reference check - Criminal Record Check - Digital footprint check - Financial history check Re-validation every 15 years	5 years
Negative Vetting 1	Same as above but with ASIO assessment. Re-validation every 10 years	10 years
Negative Vetting 2	Same as above with additional requirements of security interview Re-validation every 7 years (Equivalent to TOP SECRET)	10 Years
Positive Vetting	All of the above and includes additional vetting of: - Average fortnightly expenditure - Financial probity check - Details of overseas relatives and nature of contact - Social memberships - Psychological assessment Annual security appraisal	Full life background check

Linkedin search

Typical searches in Liinkedin will give some results but very little of PV personnel who are the hardest to find and hire.

Some clearance specific key word searches you can utilize are:

"Security clearance" OR "security cleared" OR "positive vetting" OR "PV clearance" OR "PV cleared" OR "Baseline Clearance" OR NV1 OR NV2 OR "negative vetting"" OR "Top secret" OR TSPV OR "Top secret PV"

9.5 EU perspective

EU has 4 levels of clearance

- Restricted
- Confidential
- Secret
- Top Secret

Sourcing EU cleared folks

A following query can be utilized for a start in Linkedin search box or through an X-ray of Linkedin:

"EU Secret" OR "EU Restricted" OR "EU Confidential" OR "EU TOP SECRET" OR "EU Security clearance"

Since EU consists of 27 member states, the names of clearance levels are spelled in the specific member state's official language. You can utilize it to expand your search. To illustrate it further:

In Slovak Republic, the equivalent native word is "Vyhradené" for Restricted.

Likewise "Dôverné for confidential, Tajné for Secret and "Prísne tajné" for Top Secret.

Another avenue is look up EU specific agencies which most likely would need security clearances to work and handle information. Some examples are as follows:

- European Network and Information Security Agency
- European Defence Agency
- European Union Satellite Centre
- European Banking Authority
- European Border and Coast Guard Office
- European Commission
- European Space Agency

Also specific systems access of "European Travel Information and Authorisation system (ETIAS), require some form of clearance. Likewise, compile different system names and run searches along those lines.

Chapter 10 Job Description

JD's are a conversation starter, provide a glimpse of a firm and allow the candidate to imagine working for you. In the end it is all about experience, CX nonetheless.

Employers try to tell their employees to have razor sharp focus on customers but may neglect that a candidate can be an inbound customer or an outbound customer sooner or later.

Most of the job descriptions for a particular role are generic and with little understanding of how candidates perceive a JD, and in essence, the company, thru its lens.

You may wonder as to why a bid manager should worry about a JD. The best Proposal output comes from selecting the right personnel and the bid manager should take initiative in forming the outline of the job description with the real skills and success criteria for the role and let the recruiter expand on it to make it publish worthy.

A great Job Description needs to be short and sweet, clearly describes what's expected, a positive language devoid of adjectives and superlatives.

According to Harvard Business Review, Forbes, McKinsey, Women in general may not respond to Job advertisements which are long and unless they meet all the qualifications of the job.

It may be worthwhile to not have too many skill requirements and concentrate on the most important ones for the candidates to be qualified to apply for a job role.

There are a few solutions in the market which may help in developing a gender neutral job description and / or also provide readability feedback.

Gender Decoder - Free tool which points out the words which are masculine or too feminine and you can change the words to ensure gender neutral description

JobLint - Free tool which you can use to paste the job description, and check for issues with sexism, culture, expectations, and recruiter fails.

DirectlyApply – Provides a free D&I checker for job descriptions. Requires a corporate email and phone number to check

Text Analyzer - Free software utility which allows you to find the most frequent phrases and frequencies of words. Non-English language texts are supported. It also counts number of words, characters, sentences and syllables. Also calculates lexical density.

Textio - predictive engine uses a combination of natural language processing and data mining to find the words and phrases that are statistically likely to create an imbalance between the number of men and women who are inspired to respond to your job ad today and prompts you with words to change it.

It has a provision to have a database of all JDs and finds the language that best represents your company's distinct values and culture.

BeApplied - It detects problematic phrases and words and also has a feature of reading burden test and has data on the real time performance of your roles from a diversity perspective.

OnGig - OnGig's Text Analyzer software gets rid of all bias in your job postings and optimizes your text so that passive candidates engage with you

Talvista - Subscription based software featuring text refinement editor, elevated word replacements that generate a neutral and non-bias reaction, blind resume review module automatically redacts applicant names, addresses, and educational institutions from within the original resume format as well as an easy-to-use solution to create an interview script with defined structure for interviewers to quickly follow

TapRecruit - Subscription software that provides language guidance and, more importantly, content guidance via augmented writing, so your hiring teams can write job descriptions that encourage qualified candidates to apply regardless of their gender, ethnicity, or background.

JobWriter – They allow the employer to create enhanced postings don't just describe jobs, they tell the story about their goals, organization's culture, and what it genuinely feels like to work in a particular job.

Microsoft's Word 2019 version claims to apply artificial intelligence to recommend users to write in a way that does not discriminate against a particular gender. The software also uses AI to recommend synonyms and ways to shorten sentences to ensure brevity.

10.1 How to write effective Job Description

- To sound cool, exciting, trendy, and desire to showcase its a happening place, recruiters/HR can go overboard and use words such as kickass, superstar, rock star, megastar, ninja, guru, "growth hacker", "thought leader", outspoken, champion, challenger, geek, nerd, techie, evangelist, droid, drone, junkie, enthusiast, pirate, "purple squirrel", Sherpa, prophet, warrior, demigod, Jedi, Alchemist, Badass, challenger, prima donna, diva, wizard etc. which may likely turn off women or some men as well, and employers would have lost many qualified candidates as such.

- Industry buzzwords / jargon are the absolute killer. Optimize, conceptualize, synergies, hit the ground running, unicorn, competitive salary, salary commensurate with experience, industry's best salary, "salary not a constraint for the right candidate". These do not provide any glimpse of how the company functions and may give a distinct impression of a firm with little knowledge of market realities.

- Negative words usage is an absolute no-no. Common usage of these words include strict, must, cannot, will not, do not, always, unable, never etc.

- Quite a few job descriptions (especially government related) list mandatory skills apart from desired skills. Key is to not to mix them up and list the most preferred skills in the desired skills section if you absolutely have to. Try to keep it to 1-2 bullet points at the maximum for preferred skills.

- There are several occasions of a job title or role with strange wordings that a candidate may not relate with. Little creativity does work but going overboard does not help most of the time. Examples include "Digital Prophet", "chief cheerleader", "sales ninja", and "marketing genius". When a candidate runs a search, more likely such a role may not even show up in the results.

- It may be useful to minimize or eliminate boring, ad nauseam and Cliché words usage like passionate, detail oriented, multi-tasking, fast paced, results oriented, team player, excellent communication skills, self-starter, self-confident, hardworking, motivated, self-reliant, superior, compete etc. Almost every job requires such traits in an individual. There is no differentiation between one JD and another. The candidate would most likely skip over such roles as it is not an attention grabber.

- There are a few occasions of job titles with levels (Level 1 or Level 3) that a prospective candidate has no idea of. The levels are internal to a firm and the corporate messaging there may not send a good message across. Instead consider, having a job title which says junior developer, intermediate systems administrator with the relevant role descriptions and NOT like the ones below.

    Designation – Proposal Writer, Level 1

    Level 3 Proposal Writer, Cloud

- Some jobs contain too many words in the job title and it may not receive good click through most of the time. The key is to have a short job title (first one below) and **NOT** like the ones after that.

    Sample role titles:

    Proposal Writer

    Proposal Writer - II - Supply Intelligence Team

    Proposal Writer (2+ Yrs Exp) – Cloud, Infrastructure

- Utilize optimistic words in the JD, and steer clear of any pessimistic word setup, to appeal to the candidate's emotional state. We all like to be wooed but hate to be sold.

- It is important to clearly enunciate the purpose behind the work role and the culture fit that comes into play as increasingly Millennials and Gen Z are looking for evidence of it. Enough care should be taken to pinpoint any unique aspects of the position and explain what is in it for them and how it dovetails with the company's mission statement.

- An employer may not give a great impression by having syntax, formatting, spelling errors and irrelevant information in a job posting. It shows the lack of attention to detail and it would be advisable for at least another individual in the team to cross-check before publishing it.

- It is natural for an employer to expect an all-rounder (in cricket parlance) with every skill imaginable for a role but it is very unrealistic and can be counter-productive for the team. There may be no room for such an individual to learn and they may leave shortly even if they get hired. It may be worthwhile to avoid asking for everything under the sun in the JD. The key is to get the person with the right attitude having decent skills, and who can be provided opportunities to up-skill.

- Nowadays most of the job searches happen on mobile devices and being the nature of the beast, it is absolutely critical to optimize the JD for the individual to click. There are a lot of distractions and attention span is a challenge. Hence, long winding sentences and paragraphs will most likely ensure passing over the role. Key is to ensure the scrolling is minimized to a very large extent.

- It may be okay to describe for an employer to state that they have great culture, benefits and work life balance, but where is the proof?   "Show", rather than "tell" should be the mantra. It would be worthwhile to indicate for ex: we provide work from home option once every week or a fortnight or have social events every month or every Friday afternoon is a learning session etc.

- Everything has a template nowadays, including the JD for several roles. Sometimes the old phrases and responsibilities are re-used again and again with no checks on whether those still apply and strong candidates are quite quick to spot such inertia and skip these job roles altogether

- There are a lot of job postings that may sound reasonable to apply but do not have the salary range, exact work location details, special physical requirements (load/unload 40 Kg boxes etc.), shift policies, working hours, relocation support etc.

    Transparency is coveted and candidates can quickly gauge whether it is something they should go further in applying for it. Salary range for very senior roles may not be provided due to competitive reasons but for other lower levels, it may be worthwhile to indicate a range.

- Quite a few JDs one may come across in the marketplace contain a slew of responsibilities and skills requirements. Having such a long JD, an employer likely has failed to deliver a vision / dream of the role to the prospective candidate.

Example of a JD for a Proposal Writer, to the point and minimalistic

We are a leading provider of a full range of protection, control and measurement solutions - enabling safer and smarter electricity flow from substation to the point of consumption. We deliver products and systems designed to connect, protect and control electrical systems, ensuring reliability, efficiency and safety for equipment and personnel.

Reporting to the Inside Sales and Technical Proposal Manager and using your technical and customer service skills and knowledge, you will help solve diverse customer inquiries in support of the wider Technical excellence and Marketing team.

Responsibilities:

- Work collaboratively with the business development team to write, organize, format and compile commercial proposals
- Create and manage the inventory of proposal material Work with internal teams to prepare generic materials for use in proposals
- Support the marketing team in the development of marketing materials Provide on-going marketing research and other duties as assigned
- Work with a team of skilled engineers, designers, procurement and construction specialists, contractors, vendors and other project support staff/stakeholders.
- Coordinates, with technical leads, the preparation of marketing documents and proposals Develop strategic business development plan for assigned division of responsibility.

Requirements:

- Bachelor's degree or equivalent, ideally in marketing or business from a recognized college or university. Engineering or
- Technical background is considered an asset 5+ years of experience in technical, marketing and proposal writing
- Strong project management skills. Some working experience in a consulting firm providing services to utilities, engineering, power plants or other industrial projects is an asset

Chapter 11 Staffing your team

There are several ways to staff your team. Below are few examples of it.

The intake meeting with the hiring manager ("bid manager" in this case) for a proposal writer requisition usually ends with "who do you know that we can call upon".

The bid manager can provide the recruiter the following search string

("proposal specialist" OR "proposal writer" OR "proposal author" OR "Proposal development" OR "proposal developer" OR "proposal advisor" OR "proposal analyst" OR "Bid writer") to use in Linkedin and narrow it by location.

Alternatively an X-ray string to search LI thru Google to start with is illustrated below:

site:in.linkedin.com/in ("proposal specialist" OR "proposal writer" OR "proposal author" OR "Proposal development" OR "proposal developer" OR "Bid writer" OR "proposal analyst") Bangalore -job –jobs

Additionally you can add (APMP OR Shipley) to the string.

11.1 Slideshare

Anyone uploading their resume to Linkedin by default goes to Slideshare (owned by Linkedin).

This is how you can find their resumes

site:slideshare.net (Resume OR CV OR Vitae OR "curriculum vitae") "bid manager" -"resume writing"

11.2 Emoji and symbol search

Many Linkedin or profiles on Google have the special symbols of phone like this ☎ | ✆ | ☏

An X-ray search as illustrated below can be utilized to pull up profiles of individuals with phone or email symbols.

site:in.linkedin.com/in "☏" OR "☎" OR "✆" OR "✉" OR "□" -intitle:☏ -intitle:☎ -intitle:✆ -intitle:✉ devops Bengaluru area, india

You could search for cloud engineers by using Cloud emoji ☁ as well.

An example search would be site:linkedin.com/in ☁ bangalore

The following website provides Unicode characters for several emojis used in the marketplace

https://blog.emojipedia.org/whats-new-in-unicode-13-0/?fbclid=IwAR1Rjp-QjQO66ZVujbROkrBXuzGAxZyLJEkP7fXo-vaxf0A4XnTCRUxZ5rQ

11.3 APMP Awards

The APMP 40 Under 40 awards program recognizes professionals who have already made a noticeable impact on the bid management profession.

From 2017, APMP is releasing the list of award recipients and they are an excellent avenue to find prospective candidates for your team. It's a gold mine of information as you not only get a good understanding of why they received the award and also little known tidbits of information that you can utilize to do the initial outreach.

https://www.apmp.org/page/40Under40

Chapter 12 Bid management discipline

12.1 Executive summary tips

When clients request proposals for their RFPs, the bid responses that are received have 90% similar descriptions of their capabilities, experiences, staff strengths etc. It is the 10% differentiation which will decide who will bag the deal in the end.

The differentiation (a compelling Value proposition) could range from better delivery modes, better pricing models, better tool set, awards, Case studies, third party validation from research firms etc., first to the market, higher ROI and it should correlate with meeting or exceeding strategic and tactical business outcomes the customer needs, and all of this should be tied to risk, cost and time.

The executive summary is the best place to showcase the differentiation and it should flow through the entire proposal (section summary, graphics etc.) where necessary.

Here are some things to watch out for while developing an executive summary. Decision makers love to buy but hate to be sold.

- Beware of using pre written content. Consider starting from scratch.
- Don't rewrite what is in the RFP to describe your understanding of the project and the solution for it
- Talk about strengths, similar projects (lower risk)
- Customer value proposition (ROI, quantifiable benefits, efficiency)
- Focus only on customer hot buttons
- Avoid bragging (ex: greatest, best in class)
- Due care to avoid errors in grammar, punctuation and spelling

- Avoid aggressive, pushy and sales oriented word choices
- Revise to get it right but do not go overboard
- If possible, limit it to 1-2 pages. (Exceptions being large proposals)
- Write in active voice, and use a positive construct
- Keep the paragraphs short (maximum 5 lines) and one topic per paragraph
- Avoid conditional word usage (ex: If, except, unless, otherwise)
- Include relevant visuals, text only summary is passé

12.2 KPIs for a bid manager

A bid manager submits a lot of proposals to the end customers on a regular basis and it is a bone of contention to know the KPIs that are to be assigned to assess the performance of a bid manager. Here are some of them which I feel would be a good indicator of success.

- Number of proposals submitted

- Total Win rate %

- Win rate % on must win deals

- Win rate % on small (<$10M), medium($11-100M) and large deals ($100M+)

- Win rate % by financial value

- Mean proposal Aging: (from the date of proposal submission deadline)

- Proposal to presentation ratio : The number of proposals that resulted in a client presentation

- Elimination % : Number of bids that got eliminated at the evaluation stage due to compliance issues (Ideally zero)

- % of bids that received a high proposal rating from the client's side: (Mostly applicable for Government bids)

- % of bids that got submitted with less than 33% win probability and win ratio for it

- % of bids that got submitted with more than 33% win probability and win ratio for it

12.3 Account manager relationship with bid manager

When a bid manager receives an RFP from a specific client, they are either delighted or not so enthused about working on it. Does it have to do anything with client account manager relationship?

Any bid manager worth their salt would extend themselves or give their absolute everything to work with a specific client account manager. What could be the secret?

A very strong client account manager will:

- Pre sell the opportunity to a very minute level and gives all the ammunition for a bid manager to capture it extremely well in the proposal.

- Keep the loop with the bid manager on upcoming must-win opportunities and the strategies to succeed.

- Not waste a bid manager's time on needless pursuits

- Inform the bid manager to provide an obligatory client request proposal (for optics purpose and keep other vendors happy in Pre-qualified roster list)

- Understands the bid team's work load and will not over extend them to burnout

- Have a fabulous understanding of the company and its offerings and the areas where the offerings need to be customized for clients

- Command respect from the clients, peers and co-workers

- Communicate the value of your offerings from a strategic and financial perspective in a easy to understand method and with a high degree of confidence

- Treat the bid manager team as a vital cog in their goal achievements and has excellent working relationship

All said and done, any bid manager would love to talk about their wins and if a specific client account manager gets them to win more, naturally the proposal writers under their wing are more wired to work on such bids.

12.4 Proposalitis

After every quarter, the unrelenting stream of RFPs begins to roll in and the bid managers, proposal writers come under tremendous pressure to churn out proposals like a machine. In the final analysis, the bid management team has an extremely direct and major impact on many a firm's growth prospects.

After 7-10 years, quite a few bid managers and proposal writers will see a bunch of text and images floating around and questioning themselves and the field of work itself, and thinking whether it is all worth in the end.

Enter proposalitis, a state of mind specific to proposal industry exhaustion that has a serious impact on the health and wellness of the individuals.

From my personal experience, there have been many days working till 3 AM to deliver things on time and many other days burning the midnight oil.

It is just a matter of time before the mind and body shuts down and errors start creeping in unbeknownst to you.

Following are some of the things the industry can provide attention to prevent industry prevent burnout and also mine the vast knowledge accumulated:

- Reducing the number of proposals to be assigned to the team in the first place by spending more resources upfront to pre sell the solution so that the instances of blind bidding and responding to RFPs, with no selling at all, are reduced to a bare minimum.

- Qualifying the RFPs to a very granular level by completing bid win probability assessments.

- Consider introducing proposal automation to avoid to-and-fro emails, for better collaboration, better version control and thereby reducing admin activities

- Instituting better process for the proposal creation and a well-structured proposal library and reusable asset database that can be easily searched and gives relevant results

- Create a health and wellness support group and explain the benefits of exercising every day to relieve the accumulated stress and tension and the employees following the regimen. A 20 minute workout can do wonders and can re-energize sore muscles and mind.

- Go for cross-functional level assignments for 1-2 months. (I had the opportunity to do Talent acquisition alongside bid management and the dual role stayed and it helped me to better focus).

12.5 Incumbency – Advantage or a burden

Every year, there will be a spate of renewal contracts being put out to bid. The research community tracks these contracts and the vendors salivate at the prospect of unseating the incumbent while at the same time being wary of being dislodged from their own renewal contracts.

Incumbency losses can be a heart burn for many of those handling the current contracts. The days of automatic renewals have gone past and clients are seeking value driven deals while driving the cost down and are not afraid of transitioning to new vendors. Some of the circumstances and mitigation for the losses are:

- The feeling that only you know what is best for the client and the resulting complacent attitude

- A frequent source of frustration with incumbents is change requests and its financial implications to the client. If you as a vendor nickel and dime them all the time, expect a backlash at critical juncture of a renewal (Account manager's bonuses tied to the number of change requests being raised is a thorny issue)

- The incumbent putting a lot of emphasis about the current work rather than focussing on the RFP which may have a significant deviation from the current state.

- Sometimes the incumbent does not want to continue this engagement due to various reasons. Instead of terminating the contract, they just wait for the contract to expire and take no part in the subsequent bid or put a high cost bid.

- There is a change of guard at the decision making level. CEO, CIO, business sponsors, all may have moved out by the time of renewal. The incoming management may not like your firm or have their own favourites from their previous experience. The account managers have their task cut out to restart building the relationship with the new management in town.

- Expectation of cost reduction in renewal deals. Proposing cost reducing ideas and efficiency improvements maybe the way forward.

- Have a continuous capture strategy in place and always find out how the customer's vision is evolving, where they see you in the picture as a trusted and reliable vendor, and how you can help in meeting their goals

- Highlighting the staff continuity and retention programs sends a strong indicator that you are a minimal risk to the client compared to others.

- Keep a close eye on the competitors as they also will be talking to your clients with their differentiators. They are hungry, motivated and do not have the baggage of the incumbent who knows the ground realities. All you have is first-hand knowledge of the customer, their likes and dislikes, motivations and build the appropriate win themes and treat the renewal opportunity as a new bid.

12.6 Are RFPs a noose or a necklace?

There are so many bid opportunities floating around that even for a very large and extremely efficient firm, it is impossible to know of every possible opportunity that is out there or that might come out soon.

Every potential client does not list their bid opportunities on commercial websites like www.biddingo.com, www.merx.com, www.rfpdb.com, www.bidnet.com and many private sector clients bid opportunities are invitation only. What are you supposed to do? Your BD teams and other sources would funnel or inform the bid team/sales team of potential opportunities 3-12 months in advance.

Contrary to perception, many clients would love their vendors to provide some sort of assistance.

Ex:: If they wish to implement a portal or an ECM, they would love to receive a business requirements document and to hand-hold them to narrow specific requirements which apply to their business and also may need assistance to provide them a high level budget estimation of the project cost from end to end, advice in terms of risks to cover and being ready from their end to have adequate internal resources, infrastructure upgrades etc.).

There are clues to look in the RFP/RFQs which can guide you in terms of making a Bid or No-Bid decision. Either looking at the way the RFP is structured or through your bid intelligence team, you have come to the conclusion that it is an incumbent bid.

If it is a client whom you wish to work with, sometimes it may be worthwhile to provide a "LOSER" bid (depending on the project size and the cycles available to spend time on providing a response) on the expectation of showing your capabilities and experience to stand a better chance in future bids by meeting the client in person and learning about upcoming opportunities much earlier.

Also, it may be worthwhile to check if the client really wants the incumbent back.

Following are some of the issues to be aware of:

- The over confidence that the client cannot do without you and only you know the client's issues extremely well

- Some slippage in service levels

- Overly ambitious in raising change requests for very small tasks and consequent additional billing, could be an opportunity for the competitor to squeeze the Incumbent out.

- A known devil is better than an unknown devil may not work out all the time for an incumbent's thinking process.

If you have decided not to do a bid, it is important to provide a nicely crafted letter clearly explaining the reasons (avoid a generic reason) and also propose to help them in their endeavor by scheduling a phone call with them. You want to be seen as a helpful vendor even in adverse circumstances.

If you have decided that the company should pursue a bid, care needs to be taken to ensure the questions are framed to get clarifications but not expose your bid tactical strategy. Bid meetings in person and/or the phone must be attended and review the vendors that have expressed an interest.

Within the first few days, you will narrow down the list to 3-5 vendors who are most likely to respond. Assess their strengths, check if they have previous experience in working with this client, how long ago it was, did they have a good relationship etc.

Right from the sponsor, legal, contracts management, SMEs, bid response writer, marketing team are to be involved in the entire proposal response process. It is absolutely critical that your response should completely align with the evaluation criteria and its relative weighting. Analyze if you need partners to bolster your bid. Have teaming agreements in place.

Writing an executive summary (1-2 pages) is an art in itself. You have to provide a good understanding of the client's issues or needs, how your solution or service can help them in achieving their goals, your experience in providing similar work products, success stories.

The language used should be very easy to read and understand even for an 8th grader and jargons should be completely avoided.

Many of the decision makers only read your executive summary and if that is not appealing, your proposal may not get a second look or they may just skim through other sections of the proposal and consequently you have lost their attention and the end result would be very less scores.

For the rest of the proposal, identify the win themes, specific differentiators, pricing models, templates and include corporate project summaries which closely align with the scope statement. If possible, add customer quotes for similar projects you may have undertaken.

Adequate care must be taken to ensure that you do not give chance for the bid evaluation teams to knock you out of the competition.

Typical examples include:

- Signing the proposal in Black colour instead of Blue ink (this happens)

- Non-acknowledgement of the addenda

- Adding corporate brochures when it is clearly indicated not to submit

- Using your own address format instead of the client specified format

- Not referencing each evaluation criteria in your proposal

- Not limiting the response to specified page limits as stated in the RFP etc.

12.7 Are the RFPs wired?

Every medium size / large size private firm and all Public sector organizations release RFP/RFQ or go for an invitation only method to identify partners for their business and technology needs.

RFPs are a risk to the company in terms of reputation and finances, however, good risk mitigation management practices, shall significantly increase your success ratio, and avoids a lot of problems later on.

If you have a 2 in 5 winning ratio for RFPs, you are doing something very well.

If you have heard of an opportunity after the RFP is released, you have most likely lost the plot. From my personal experience, 70% of the RFPs are pre-sold by another vendor or an incumbent is present, and this elaborate process is undertaken to give an impression to their internal stakeholders or to the Vendor community that they are being fair and are doing the due diligence.

To be fair to the client community, they are trying to reduce their risk with a known entity or a trusted advisor in their opinion. I have won blind bids but it is a tough ask to win.

No one gets recognition for standing second unlike an Olympics 2nd place finish. It impacts the firm's staff members from a motivation perspective. Defeats can be contagious and no matter what lessons learned and debriefings you may attend, loss is a loss.

However, there are certain instances where an incumbent / preferred vendor has failed or unable to deliver, a 2nd placed vendor may get a chance to get on the project but there are different risks altogether for such a scenario.

There are tell-tale signs to watch out for the RFPs that are most likely wired from the get-go.

- The proposal length, excluding staff resumes and collateral, shall not exceed 20-25 pages unless it is a Pre-qualification to shorten the list of applicants to a manageable number of 5-10 for follow-up bids for specific opportunities.

- There are specific requirements of having a pre-existing local office and service response times of 5-10 minutes.

- Very little information is provided in the bid document and subsequent Q&A provides very little clarity on the scope, deliverables and deadlines.

- Bid response submission deadlines are unrealistic (How about 2 weeks?) To actually know for sure there is an incumbent, ask for a deadline extension of 2-4 weeks and if the request is declined, you have confirmed the fears. It is standard to have a 4-12 week time-frame to respond depending on the scope statement.

- The over anxiousness of the client in calling the vendors to see if they will be responding. For audit purposes, almost all clients need 3 bids at a minimum.

- The evaluation weightage towards pricing is quite high (40% and above) or more than 50% for the vendor staff experience and past performance.

- Unusual specifications or experience working on a specific system only an incumbent can meet

- A prototype of the system is to be provided along with the bid. The incumbent has already the demo in place and you may be giving free ideas to your competitor in providing a bid in such situations.

- Proposal references threshold is abnormally high or very specific. Ex: For Staffing services preferred Vendor RFP; bid documents stated the requirement of 3-5 references providing 100 consultants per year and total billings of 25 million dollars each within the last 2 years.

- Some RFPs say the bid document was developed by a consulting firm. Ask if they are allowed to bid on the solution or product delivery as well.

- During the bidders meeting session, you notice the absence of the competitors you have expected to attend as well as usual suspects, which should give a clue to you that something is amiss.

- The responses to the Questions are so brief or overwhelmingly complex.

- The requirement that the resumes of the staff that are proposed should be available when the project begins and cannot be substituted unless the individual leaves the firm.

- An RFP where a product firm is bidding from your intelligence and you being a partner for implementing their products at other clients is a competitor in this instance.

- RFP states the incumbent resources cannot be hired by the winning vendor other than the incumbent due to non-compete and non-solicitation clauses in their contracts.

Also review the bid document properties and see who the author is and cross-reference it to see if it is written by another vendor's staff.

In certain circumstances like IT application maintenance projects or everyday consumables in the private sector, price is the major decisive factor.

In spite of the presence of an incumbent, it would be worthwhile to submit a bid. Also, a few private sector clients will not invite a Vendor who shall not submit a credible bid, for future requirements.

Also for many large Defence Procurements of $10 billion and above, there are only 2-3 vendors who can actually deliver.

In such circumstances Government will pay the Vendor for the reasonable cost of preparing a proposal. However, since the stakes are so high, only a deep relationship and fantastic bid response with a reasonable price can get you the nod.

In the end, it is about the cycles available for the bid team as well as the commitment from the upper management that can play an important role in making a Bid or No-bid decision.

12.8 Words and Phrases to avoid in business Proposals

Business Proposals are directed towards client reviewers and decision makers.

In the eagerness to describe how great a firm is or how they are the perfect partner, the proposal writers may insert some unnecessary words that may damage the credibility of the response itself or expose the company to unknown legal liabilities.

Following are some of the words and phrases you might wish to avoid in RFP responses:

Industry buzzwords or jargon

Optimize	Leverage	Conceptualize
Synergies	Hit the ground running	Bells and whistles
Seamless	Back of the envelope	Game changer
Ideation	Paradigm shift	Low hanging fruit
Reinvent the wheel	Secret Sauce	Silver bullet
Test the waters	Holistic	Operationalize
Incentivize	Customer centric	Democratize
Thinking outside the box	Smoke and mirrors	Raising the bar
Hard and fast	Last but not the least	

Fancy / Adjective / Superlative words

Kickass	Superstar	Rock star
Ninja	Guru	Growth hacker
Thought leader	Champion	Challenger
Geek	Nerd	Techie
Evangelist	Junkie	Enthusiast
Pirate	Purple squirrel	Sherpa
Prophet	Warrior	Demigod
Jedi	Alchemist	Diva
Unicorn	Wizard	Fastest, Highest

Slang words

Killing it	Crushing it	Kick the tires
Where the rubber meets the road	Bang for the buck	Skin the cat

Boastful words or phrases

World class	Best in class	Industry leading
Unmatched	Best of breed	State of the art
Highest quality	Unparalleled	Unique
Top quality	Unsurpassed	Superior
Cutting edge	Bleeding edge	

Confidence killing words or phrases

Try	Hope	Hopefully
Can	We may	Maybe
Might	Anxious	Confident
We believe	Belief	Strive
We think	We feel	We intend

Legal risk words or phrases

Assure	Ensure	Insure
Guarantee	Best efforts	Trusted Partner
Will meet / exceed your requirements	Highly reliable	

Attention capturing words or phrases

Full scale review	Thoroughly	Meticulous
Extremely certain	Fine-comb	Precise

Other words or phrases

We are committed	We are pleased	We are happy
We are delighted	We understand	However
Therefore	Peel the onion	Linchpin
Weed out	Baked into	Trustworthy
Circle back	Touch base	Marinate the idea

Redundant words

There are different types of redundant words such as:

- Acronym additions
- Modifying an adjective
- Symbol expansion
- Using 2 or more words that serve the same purpose
- Overusing adverbs or using an adverb to modify a verb

A few examples are explained below:

- Company X will contribute €10 Million Euro towards improving infrastructure of a school for the physically handicapped - € is symbol for Euro and repeating it in words is redundancy.

- I have been guilty of using them from time to time - using time twice is redundancy - instead use "a few times"

- We have an install base of 300 ATM machines - Remove ATM machines and instead use 300 ATM's.

- It is absolutely critical that the change requests are signed off by both parties before starting work on them - Absolutely is an emphasis word used in this context when it is not necessary.

- Other than country X, Y that have their own space navigation systems, no other country has managed to develop it - It seems perfectly fine for a casual reader. Removing "other" in the 2nd instance may make it sound a little better but if you were to rewrite it as "X and Y are the only countries that have a space navigation system", it is much easier to read and follow.

Following are some redundant words and its replacements

Original word	Replacement
The issue at hand	The issue
Absolutely required	Required
End result	Result
Plan ahead	Plan
As a result	Because
Having said that	However
Each and every	Every
In the event that	If
Past experience	Experience
As of yet	Yet
Browse through	Browse
Critically important	Important
Few in number	Few
Free gift	Gift
Merge together	Merge
Proceed further	Proceed
Slight edge	Edge
Well respected	Well regarded

Additionally, proposal writers may subconsciously develop their responses with specific gender in mind (habitual reasons) and they are better off writing with being more inclusive.

Some classic examples of word usage and its replacements are listed below:

Original word	Replacement word
Man	Person
He/him/she/her	They, them
His, hers, his or hers, his/her	Their
Mankind	Humanity
Manpower	Workforce or personnel
Manmade	Manufactured or Machine-made
Chairman or chairwoman	Chairperson or chair
Policeman or Policewoman	Police officer
Miss/Mrs	Ms.
Spokesman	Spokesperson
Guys or gals	Folks or everyone
Steward or stewardess	Flight attendant
Common man	Average individual
Sir/Madam/Madame	Use the actual name if you know
Man-hours	Staff-hours
Businessman/businesswoman	Business executive
Handicapped, disabled, physically challenged	Individual with a specific disability
Forefathers	Ancestors
Gunman or gunwoman	Shooter
Fireman	Firefighter
Landlord	Owner
Salesman	Sales representative or salesperson
Postman	Postal worker
Middleman	Intermediary
Draftsman	Drafter
Craftsman	Artisan
Foreman	Supervisor
Housewife	Homemaker
Maid	House cleaner
Alderman	Council member
Master's degree	Post Graduate degree
Masterpiece	A great work of art
Lumberjack	Logger
Headmaster	Principal

Gender neutral language guidelines in European Parliament

https://www.europarl.europa.eu/cmsdata/151780/GNL_Guidelines_EN.pdf

UN Gender Inclusive Language Guidelines

https://www.un.org/en/gender-inclusive-language/guidelines.shtml

12.9 Word spellings to look for in business Proposals

United States is probably the single biggest software product and services market in the World. While drafting proposals, a non-US resident individual can frequently notice specific words that MS-Word flags with a red underline (potential incorrect spelling). They are not misspelt by any means but American English words are usually shortened or have different pronunciations.

Following are some of the examples:

"Or" verses "Our"

US Specific	Non US Specific
Behavior	Behaviour
Color	Colour
Endeavor	Endeavour
Favor	Favour
Flavor	Flavour
Honor	Honour
Labor	Labour
Rigor	Rigour
Rumor	Rumour

"er" versus "re"

US Specific	Non US Specific
Caliber	Calibre
Center	Centre
Fiber	Fibre
Meager	Meagre
Meter	Metre

"ense" versus "ence"

US Specific	Non US Specific
Defense	Defence
License	Licence
Offense	Offence

"ize" versus "ise"

US Specific	Non US Specific
Analyze	Analyse
Organize	Organise
Realize	Realise
Recognize	Recognise

Other words

US Specific	Non US Specific
Artifact	Artefact
Check	Cheque
Gray	Grey

Under File > Options > Language, you can add your language of choice of editing a document to avoid this minor inconvenience.

12.10 Persuasive writing

Imagine the procurement or decision making team quickly skimming your proposal and yawn. It happens a lot more than you think. It only means that the proposal being reviewed has not hit the mark in persuasive writing standards.

Following are some of the tips you could potentially utilize:

- Convert most of the sentences to an active voice (there is a place for passive voice too).

- Avoid adding a lot of text. Leave some white space after 2-3 lines especially in areas where you want to navigate the reader to focus more closely.

- Utilize trigger words like because, difference, investment, imagine but do not overuse them. Back that up with data if you are using more than once or twice in your proposal.

- Try to limit your bullet points to "Three" or "Four" to illustrate a benefit or anything else relevant for the reader to process better and remember it afterwards.

- Where possible, try to limit the words in a sentence to 20 words or less

12.11 Proposal Quality Validation

A consulting firm or a product firm with services division annually bids on a number of projects. The sales personnel would ideally like the proposal development team to bid on a lot of initiatives to maximize chances of a sale, but the bandwidth of the proposals team is limited. .

The Bid - No bid decision meetings can be a very testing time, with everyone voicing their opinions and the commercials/pursuit heads finally making a decision.

Once an initiative is given the green light to proceed, the validation of proposal quality comes to the fore. The validation should be performed by someone other than the authors of the document.

Here are a few items that need to be paid attention to:

Typographical, contextual and copying errors: Spell check alone cannot identify errors. A proper word like "intimate" (usually used in an Indian writing context) is a perfectly acceptable word but it has different connotations and shall be replaced by "inform". Other incorrectly spelt words like Public, Manager or Managerial can cause lot of anguish.

Likewise, having other client names or words reflecting different projects are copied and oversight may happen, resulting in embarrassments.

Also the spelling of the word "Color", "meager", "favorable" is acceptable for US bids but may not be suitable for other jurisdictions.

Assumptions: Every proposal's solution and pricing is based on certain documented assumptions. Whether these assumptions are warranted and necessary or are they over the top scaring a potential customer.

Customer centric: Quite a few proposals reproduce what the customer has specified in the RFP without explaining the understanding of the customer's need and explaining how your solution solves their issues. Beware of using "we understand".

Trade-offs: Like any vendor that goes through the process, the proposals have to balance out the interests of the internal stakeholder's revenue and profitability requirements, the risk appetite as well as Value add for the customer.

Compliance: Every RFP is different and hence the compliance criteria vary. Some of the criteria one should pay close attention to are:

- Total Response page limits excluding resumes, if any
- Individual sections page limits, if any
- Brochures
- Financial statements
- Certification statements (insurance, incorporation, minority owned, Tribal/Aboriginal etc.)
- Font type, font size
- Declaration statements
- Signatures in Ink
- Qualification matrices
- Number of copies (Physical and electronic)

The evaluators have their own jobs to come back to after the review process, so make it easy for them to find information in a logical sequence, minimizing external link references as much as possible and using simple to understand language and avoiding the usage of flattery and complicated word usage etc.

Win themes: Every RFP document is incomplete in some way or the other. It's not what disclosed in the RFP that can entirely change the game plan. By knowing the evaluators, the decision makers, the real pain points can be addressed effectively such that a true customer focused solution is presented.

General win themes to be found across the proposals -

- Features and benefits statements with supporting facts
- Low risk
- Outcome based pricing
- Best value for money

The selected themes shall be articulated across the entire sections of the proposal where relevant in a subtle and not so subtle ways. By following the "SHOW' rather than "TELL" method, you have proof to back up your claims.

Risk mitigation: There is a likelihood of a service provider coming up with solutions which are quite innovative but carry a lot of risk premium for the customer. It's incumbent on the vendor to understand whether the customers are risk averse or not, and then propose the solution accordingly.

Similar experience: Any customer by nature wants to select a provider who has done similar work as they are comfortable with them not being a test customer for an important internal initiative.

It is incumbent on the Vendor to provide detailed reference examples of similar work as close to the customer's need as possible with user numbers, adoption statistics, customer satisfaction surveys, positive public comments etc. to name a few.

Pricing: The proposal should account for direct, indirect, upfront commitment, in-kind contributions, investment costs, volume discounts, if any.

Resumes: The proposed team's resumes all should follow the same format. The customer is interested to see the project experiences relevant to them. It is advisable to describe them out first and then go about explaining other projects.

Why us: Structure the proposal in simple language as to why the customer should select you with all relevant facts and figures.

12.12 Client Presentations

You responded to a client RFP and received the good news of being short listed for a presentation. The entire bid team is happy but the real game begins now.

Here is how that you could make a compelling presentation without being overbearing by utilizing the following tips:

- The presentation team often wrestles with the number of slides to be prepared. Look at the time slot given, the client attendees background (procurement, tech support, architecture, business managers, finance heads etc.) as well as their business needs, motivation, influence, power, success factors etc. and prepare the slides accordingly.

- Just as how you may see a defense lawyer in US or Canadian Court present their case to a jury with an initial briefing, then go into detail, and summarize at the end on behalf of their client, you would work along the same lines for the client review team to remember 3-4 things about you that will stick in their minds while they make a decision afterwards.

- Human beings are an emotional lot with degrees of variance. Try to appeal to the audience with relevant story lines (Increased revenues or decreased % cost, lead generation % increase, % increase of enquiries to conversions, visitors trends increase etc.) to keep them interested.

- Fast talking like a snake oil salesman is an absolute no-no. Slow down.

- Only the presenters need to go to the onsite meeting, and avoid taking bench warmers or passengers. If it's a Web based presentation, only the relevant people who know the bid inside out shall make a presentation.

- Everyone has a unique way of presentation. The key is to be you, rather than pretend to be someone else while presenting.

- Don't read out the slides as it conveys nothing and maybe insulting to the audience.

- Don't pack too much text and information in the slides (the client team has read your proposal before, so no need to burden them again)

- Utilize charts, illustrations that are easy on the eye.

- If it's an onsite presentation, keep eye contact, and if possible, move around rather than stay at one spot to appeal to all the decision makers.

- If it's a digital presentation, fewer slides are better due to distraction and reduced attention span.

- Go light on the jargon as you may have a mixed audience.

- Presentations can stimulate the audience to ask questions, so it might eat into the material you were planning to present. An engaged audience is 100 times better than more slides, so adapt your presentation on the fly to cater to their needs.

- The client review team has a list of prepared questions and sometimes you may not have an answer for 1 or 2 questions (specifically legal or conflict of interest or questions that require a little more time to provide an effective answer).

Promise to get back to them with a definite timeline rather than giving an off the cuff reply which may damage your chances.

The review team just wants to clarify the concerns they had about your firm's proposal as well as feeling comfortable to deal with you. In the end it is about trusting your firm to do a good job.

12.13 Bid debriefing

You spent a large amount of time, money to provide a credible bid involving so many stakeholders but still end up on the losing side. You have researched the organization, your competitors, pricing models, did a lot of pre-selling, provided a very compelling presentation but the dreaded form letter from the client is dispiriting, to say the least.

Remember, the proposals are scored, not read.

You get angry, may even punch the desk or wall hard, fear your top management's wrath, may not be so courteous with your family after you go home. However you have another opportunity to meet with the client during a debriefing. It is important to glean as much information as possible.

A public sector debriefing can be a very standardized response and apart from irregular scoring and a clear bias towards a competitor's response, there is not a whole lot you can do other than a bid protest which can be quite costly.

If it is a private sector bid, you have a good scope to better understand where you might have fallen short, whether your assumptions were fair, and probably be better prepared to do a lot more Pre-selling ahead of the curve.

It is important to have a very calm personality and a lot of prodding to obtain the desired information.

Sometimes if you are lucky, you may even get off the record feedback which can be extremely valuable.

It is crucial to know:

- What did they like about your proposal?
- What did they not like?
- What are the areas of improvement?

Following are the items which are generally discussed:

- Did the executive summary excite the review team? If not, what was the issue?

- Was the Presentation style, content clear and concise?

- Did reviewers struggle or had no problems to find information?

- Did your proposal claim statements without facts?

- Were the Proposed team quality, relevant project experiences, and innovative response valued by the client?

- Did the proposal have the right assumptions or had too many assumptions?

- Did the pricing models had qualifiers attached potentially scaring the customer?

- Was the proposed solution optimum with little risk or was the solution not meeting the requirements (high risk, lot of fluff, too much self-praise and the like).

- Did the proposal have relevant graphics or had too much verbose, mix of active voice and passive voice?

- Were the benefits of proposal clear or not clearly laid out?

- Was there too much ghosting of your competitor's weakness or strengths?

- The proposal flow (unexplained abruptness in paragraph endings or sentences, spelling/copy paste errors, not so clear descriptions on how your firm can meet the evaluation criteria, several external links to information, too many look ups etc.)

- Scores for each section, relevant pricing models, pricing below or above their budget, how far in percentage terms were you above and below the winner from a pricing perspective.

Once you have noted down all the comments, conduct a lessons learned session with all bid stakeholders to disseminate the information and make positive changes to the entire process where necessary.

It is useful to ask for and attend a debriefing session even if you win as the evaluation panel may have noticed certain shortcomings that you can improve upon for future bids.

12.14 RFP Tricky clauses

Bid management professionals run into hundreds of RFPs annually and there are always some tricky clauses to navigate before deciding to make a bid. Some of the tricky clauses to be on the lookout are:

- Bond deposits

- Escrow agreements (Code or design or other collateral)

- Termination for convenience with 30-60 days' notice period

- E&O insurance requirements

- Only the Submitted resource profiles can work on the ensuing contract with no substitutions except in the case of the individual leaving the company or disability or death.

- Local office support requirements and a 2-4 hour turnaround time to appear in person

- Geographically restrictive clauses for litigation

- What-if-scenarios for client being acquired by others

- Price reduction clauses (especially in 5-10 year agreements)

- Conflict of interest clauses (ex: the project is for design work which states that you cannot work on future more lucrative implementation work)

- Deliverable based payment schedule

- Payment terms (90/120 days)

- Performance bank guarantee

- Dispute resolution (arbitration, rectification)

- Penalty clauses (breach of contract)

- Liquidated damages clause for delayed or undelivered deliverables (usually fixed at % of the contract value)

- Security deposit

12.15 Win Loss Analysis

In its purest form, Win Loss Analysis is basically a review of the specific criteria based sales opportunities that are won and lost, and why. It puts to rest rumours, speculation and provides the direct feedback from clients, if done the correct way.

Win Loss Analysis shall be undertaken to obtain Competitive intelligence in terms of gaining a greater understanding of competitors' product and service offerings, competitors' sales strategies, and pricing models etc. This helps in pricing the offerings more accurately relative to the competition.

Ideally, you would want to complete win loss interviews with prospects or existing clients within 4 weeks of the bid award and is kept to a maximum of 30 minutes or less.

Key things to look for while thinking of conducting a Win-Loss Analysis:

- Win loss reviews shall have a program sponsor to have meaningful success

- The reviewers shall not be from sales and marketing nor from the bidding team

- Determine the goals, desired outcomes, document the questions to ask prospective clients and decide which of these clients require outreaches.

- Engage Sales teams and obtain inputs from them in terms of the interview questions to be asked and providing Win Loss findings once the exercise is complete will ensure a closer collaboration going forward.

- The upper management requires the investment made in Win Loss analysis program to have made a difference in winning bids. So ROI figures would be very useful for program continuation.

- Document competitive pricing intelligence by obtaining relative percentage differences of pricing quotes (Upper or lower than your firm's)

- Don't expect miracles right away from the Win Loss Analysis programs. Continued focus, tuning of the questions, processes will ensure a lot of derived value for the sales and bid teams.

- Complete internal reviews before conducting client interviews

- Ensure the reviewed team is not being raked over the coals

- Document the key findings and categorize them in a knowledge management system

- Establish criteria for reviewing the deals on a quarterly or monthly basis. (Dollar value basis, BU basis, territory etc.)

- Equal number of wins and loss deals to be reviewed

- An equitable Geographic distribution of deal reviews would be very useful

- Apply the lessons learned for future bids. Example: The product team may notice certain features that were the deal breaker, which can be enhanced for better product positioning in the future.

Win Loss Analysis data can be used to assess the following among other areas:

- Total Win % Ratio

- Win Ratio by Vertical, geography

- Win Loss Ratio by Sales Rep (can be used for better training)

- Win Ratio due to marketing activity

Win Loss Interview questions

Following are some of the questions you can add to the interview questionnaire:

- What was the business problem you were trying to solve?
- Which other organizations were in the mix?
- What are your impressions of our company from the start of this bid? (Leader or innovator or follower)
- How did the sales team manage the entire process?
- What could the sales representative do better in the next interactions with you?
- How would you rate our product or service? Is there anything you liked or disliked?
- What are the top three criteria behind you choosing the Winning Vendor?
- How was the decision made?
- Did our firm customize the product or service offering to meet your needs?
- Were you able to talk to our referenced customers? What did they say about us?
- Were there any specific product or service features that were very impressive from other vendors?
- What were our strongest and weakest areas in the entire process?
- What were our competitor's strongest and weakest areas in the entire process?

12.16 Proposal Automation software requirements checklist

Introduction

Bid management teams have to wrestle with concurrent RFPs on a daily basis. Most of the companies have content or document management systems in place to handle the responses.

They do however fall short in providing insights into the whole process like content value and frequency of use, productivity, version control, monitoring review cycles, intelligent recommendation engines to suggest content edits and auto-completion of questionnaires.

Enter proposal automation software into the mix. The companies that have invested a lot of money in their ECM/EDM systems have a classic conundrum of build versus buy.

Can they extend their systems with AI components for proposal automation? They could but do they have the will, the time, capable tech resources and SMEs support to build it? The jury is out.

Following is the selection checklist for reviewing the proposal automation software solutions in the marketplace.

Company

- How long have you been in business?

- Where is your firm based out of? Do you have any offices locally?

- How many active clients do you have?

- Do you have any clients in our domain that we can speak to?

- How long has this product been on the market and operational with actual customers? How many versions have been released?

- What percentage of your firm's revenue do you invest in Research and Development?

- Are you cash positive? (If it's a private firm)

- Do you have investors? How long have they invested? Have they invested in multiple rounds? When was the latest cash infusion?

Technical requirements

- Is the solution cloud only, on-premise, or web based? Can it support Android / iOS?

- Can the solution work behind VPN?

- If its cloud only, where is the hosting centre located?

- If web based, what browsers are supported? Firefox, IE, Chrome, Opera and versions?

- Is it a fully native AI solution or does it have some AI components?

Functional requirements

Proposal quality improvement

- Does the solution maintain a glossary of words and phrases that should not be present in a proposal which a writer can cross-reference?

- Does it have Geo specific problematic word highlighters? (Example: Meager is used in US but in India and Anglo-Saxon countries the correct word is "meagre". Likewise other examples are color, behavior, center which cater to US audience but may not be acceptable for a non-US audience)

- Does the solution highlight words that can be a problematic from a legal perspective (examples: insure, guarantee, promise etc.)

- Can the solution detect conditional word usage in executive summary? (examples: If, unless)

- Can the solution detect active and passive voice word usage in executive summary and other sections?

Document formats and parsing

- Can the solution allow for import and export of documents from different file formats (PDF, doc, docx, xls, slsx, wpd, Powerpoint, JPEG, PNG, GIF, Visio, PSD)

- When you upload the RFP to the solution, does it extract key information like contractual clauses for a quick read for legal department to review? Likewise, does it extract pricing related information for Commercial team to review?

- Does it capture key data like submission deadline, deadline for asking questions, number of copies to be submitted etc.?

- Can the solution annotate parsed paragraphs and sentences?

- Can the solution allow you to Search & Filter parsed paragraphs and sentences?

- Can the solution generate a Summary of the RFP?

- Can the solution extract data from imported resumes, highlights the skills specific to the RFP requirements, and then organizes information into a proposal-specific template?

Proposal productivity

- Does the solution have some sort of recommendation engine for auto-suggestions to improve productivity?

- Does the solution have the ability to present the bid participants with guideline of how a specific question has previously been answered and supporting the user to create a client specific response to each specific question?

- Quite a few RFPs have a questionnaire to be answered. If it is uploaded to the platform, can the solution pre-fill based on past responses for similar questions?

- Can the solution allow guest users to comment or provide input without logging in?

- Does the solution have in-built APMP or Shipley templates or allow new templates to be created?

Task analysis, distribution and collaboration

- How are tasks allocated to team members?

- Does the solution allow for Task notifications for new and pending tasks?

- Does the solution allow you to collaborate through Microsoft Teams, Slack, WhatsApp, SMS?

- Does the solution have a chat facility to discuss bid strategy, progress?

Search

- Can the solution support adding Meta data to the document for better search (examples such as owner, search terms, expiration date, client name, sales head). Does it support creation of custom Meta data fields?

- Does the solution allow for phrase and proximity search?

- Can you save your favourite searches so you don't have to reapply the same filters in the future?

- Can you search metadata, by title, by file type, by date created or modified?

Editing

- Does the solution have the ability to allow multiple users to comment and edit upon the same document simultaneously?

- Does the solution provide an Audit trail and document tracking of edits?

- Does the solution provide access to all prior revisions of a document?

Miscellaneous

- How is content maintenance handled?

- How does the solution support working with multiple subcontractors? How does it handle sensitive information such as financial data, and create firewalls between different subcontractors working on the same project?

- Does the solution support time zone detection for the bid team while reviewing and putting and timestamp on the edits?

- Does the solution support languages other than English?

- Does the solution allow for a word count of the response?

- Does the solution have an option to Burn to CD from within the working area?

- Can the solution support RFQs, Sole source quotations, security questionnaires?

- Does the solution support content review efforts by giving visibility into the content that is being used the most by project teams?

- Does the solution identify Long Sentences? Can they be user defined?

- Can the solution give a Readability Score for every paragraph and the 'Grade Level' required for understanding of the drafted content.

- Can the solution flag overuse of passive voice and adverbs?

- Can the solution identify differences between different versions of the same document, in terms of "addition, modification, deletion or no changes'?

- Can the solution identify incorrect and inconsistent use of acronyms?

- What is the estimated learning curve for this product?

- What features have you planned for or on the verge of implementing for the next release?

- Do you have a user group for cross-industry collaboration and support?

Integration

- Can the solution integrate with CRM and Salesforce automation systems? What are the current solutions that are currently supported?

- Does it have native integrations with Grammarly, Google Maps, Google Sheets, Google Forms, Typeform, Calendly?

- Typically, what is the timeframe required for integration with CRM/ Salesforce automation system?

General

- Does the solution allow users to create branding rules or scan proposals for brand compliance?

- Does the solution allow users to utilize proposal templates for standard proposal layouts, with variable fields?

Reporting

- What reports can your solution provide?

- Are these reports ad hoc or canned?

- Can the reports be exported to Excel or similar software?

- Does the solution have a dashboard to provide visibility into all new and pending RFP response projects?

- Does it provide information related to deadlines, progress meter, author and reviewer summaries?

- Does the solution provide Win loss pattern analysis? Can it be customized?

Security

- How is the user setup?

- What are the access privileges?

- How is the control's setup to restrict users in terms of who can view and edit elements of proposals?

- Can Permissions be set at the user, file, folder, and project workspace levels?

- Does the solution allow for password change reminders, two-factor authentication, automatic lockout after multiple failed login attempts, and automatic session timeouts?

- Does the solution support 128-256 bit AES encryption standard for two way communication?

- How is GDPR compliance handled?

- Does the solution have ISO/IEC 27001:2013 certification? Ask for SOC 2 Type 1 audit report at a minimum or even better Type 2 report under NDA from the software provider and SOC3 report from the cloud hosting provider.

- What is the impact of PATRIOT Act on your software? Is there an option to host the data locally? Can you enable it?

Support

- Do you provide 24x7x365 support from anywhere? If not, Monday-Friday 24x7?

- Do you have tiered levels of support for emergency, 1-2 hour and 1 day turnaround?

- What sort of training is available? (Webinars, in-person, on-demand, embedded?)

- Do you survey current users on the quality of the support, and if so, how frequently? If so, provide your most recent report and the report from one year prior.

Pricing Models

- Is there a setup fee?

- Is there a full featured trial option available?

- Monthly plans or annual plans or bundles?

- Is there an unlimited user's option available?

- Per user model? Minimum number of user's committment?

- Enterprise license - Based on the Number of employees?

- Are solution upgrades chargeable?

Things to look for before making a decision

Ease of use

Check if a new trial user with limited training or by just going through a demo can easily use the software to perform the following basic tasks as a starting point:

- New projects creation
- Uploading RFPs
- Editing content
- Assigning content blocks to proposal writers
- Assign Permissions for other users

If these tasks are hard to complete, it is likely that the actual users may also find it tough to use and adopt it later on.

Integration

Check if the solution has native integration APIs with Salesforce, Dynamics CRM and other popular CRMs.

If the solution does not have a native integration module, it may be preferable to implement the integration pieces once the software use is stabilized.

Content maintenance

Initially when the software is installed and used, availability of content will be less, so it would be easy to maintain.

As you start uploading a lot of previous RFPs and its related response, the responsibility on maintaining the content database becomes crucial.

The costs of content maintenance should be kept in mind.

Following is the list of Vendors that you can explore before making a decision. This is by no means an exhaustive list.

- Avnio
- Bidhive.com
- Draftspark.ai (Xerox)
- Loopio
- Qvidian
- RFPIO
- Visible Thread
- Zbizlink

12.17 Writing and Presentation tools

There are several tools in the marketplace (Some free and some are Paid versions) that improves productivity and enhances your creative abilities. Following are some examples that you can explore:

Hemingway Editor

A word processor and proofreading tool (usually used by writers) that provides:

- Readability grade
- Word count
- Adverb count
- Passive voice constructions
- Hard to read sentences and complex words or phrases.

Readable

- Provides a readability rating (Flesch - Kincaid Grade level and Gunning Fox Index)
- Word count
- Spelling and grammar issues
- Adverb and cliché count

Their paid version also provides passive voice, buzzwords, profanity and lazy words count, longest sentences by word count, adjectives, reading time etc.

ReadabilityFormulas

A free tool that allows 150-3000 words of text to be analyzed for obtaining a readability score.

ClarityGrader

Analyze any Web Page or a piece of Text, and get a FREE plain language report. An email address is required.

Tone Analyzer

It's a decent tool to analyze the tone of the text you draft in the proposals. It can also check the tone of an email message, tweet or an online review as well.

It can be used at the document level to get a sense of the overall tone of the document, as well as at the sentence level to identify specific areas of your content where tones are the strongest.

Grammarly

Compose bold, clear, mistake-free writing with Grammarly's AI-powered writing assistant and detect the tone of the writing.

ProWritingAid

A grammar checker, style editor, and writing mentor in one package. The free version has 500 word limit and online only but their paid version has no word limit, integration with MS Word, Google Docs, Chrome, and Scrivener.

Xmind

It is a mind mapping and brainstorming tool, designed to generate ideas, inspire creativity, brings productivity in a remote WFH team.

Canva

It is a graphic design platform that allows users to easily create social media graphics, presentations, posters and other visual content. It integrates millions of images, fonts, templates and illustrations.

Many of the images are paid options though.

Beautiful.ai

Create beautiful pitches and proposals in minutes and it uses AI to recommend visual elements and layouts on your slides based on design principles. Their pricing page details the differences between FREE and Pro versions.

Emaze

Build Amazing Digital Presentations very quickly. Their pricing page outlines the differences between FREE and PAID versions.

Piktochart

A web based design application that lets you create professional looking infographics, posters, reports, flyers, social media graphics, and presentations using a simple drag-and-drop interface.

It does not support native video playback on presentations, which rules out interactive presentations.

RAW Graphs

RAW Graphs is an open source data visualization framework built with the goal of making the visual representation of complex data easy for everyone.

Primarily conceived as a tool for designers and visual geeks, RAW Graphs aims at providing a missing link between spreadsheet applications (e.g. Microsoft Excel, Apple Numbers, OpenRefine) and vector graphics editors (e.g. Adobe Illustrator, Inkscape, Sketch).

12.18 Proposal Writer interview discussion points

A bid manager's deadlines and quality of proposal is fully dependent on the proposal writers under their wing. A good proposal writer can elevate the bid quality with high attention to detail, focus, communication, persuasion, compliance driven methods.

Following are some of the areas of interest a proposal writer can potentially encounter in an interview:

- What has been your greatest accomplishment so far?

- Give us couple of examples of the recent proposal sections that you wrote. How did you go about it? (Sources, research, discussions, previous proposals etc.)

- With the nature of work, you would be inundated with lot of information. How do you go about to figure out what is relevant for a specific work assignment?

- What was the recent re-usable asset you have created? What was the scope, and how did you compile this information?

- Attention to detail is one of the biggest attributes of a proposal writer. What processes and methods do you follow that nothing gets missed out in the overall output?

- Apart from collaborating with Bid manager, who do you work closely in touch for inputs to your writing assignments? How do you ensure they provide you the relevant information on time?

- Did you have experience editing content created by other writers? Where do you think the initial information fell short?

- What dependencies and factors have you considered when selecting images, charts to illustrate the subject matter effectively? A couple of examples would suffice.

- What tools do you utilize to develop graphics for the proposals? What is your preference and why?

- What are the quality metrics do you utilize the final output is clean and crystal clear with minimal revisions?

- What are some of the words you avoid using in your proposal writing assignments? Do you maintain a glossary of such words to rephrase them in case you come across them?

- You may run into different terminologies, methodologies, frameworks, product based collateral. What methods have you used to become quickly familiar with them?

- The bid teams are under tremendous pressure to obtain the maximum technical points for each proposal section and there is a temptation to stretch the truth. Give couple of examples when your ethics was tested on the job.

- Which vertical do you find it the most challenging to comply and respond? Give us a few examples.

- How many proposals did you support in the last year?

- We all have had oversight in writing assignments somewhere in our career. Can you provide couple of examples? What did you learn from it?

- What are the areas of learning you have utilized to improve your knowledge in the proposal writing area?

12.19 Bid Manager Interview discussion points

A bid manager can make or break a bid with high attention to detail, focus, communication, persuasion, compliance driven methods.

Following are some of the discussion points a Bid Manager can potentially encounter:

- In your opinion, what is the current state of the bid management discipline? Where do you think it is headed?

- What has been your greatest accomplishment so far?

- What is your opinion of Win % as a KPI for a bid manager? What metrics do you think would be most appropriate for a bid manager?

- A proposal's quality output is as good as the team in operation. Based on your experience, what are the key ingredients of a good team?

- Sales people want you to bid on every opportunity they think is worth bidding on. What's your involvement in Bid/No bid decisions and what factors do you consider while taking up bid support for a specific project?

- Give us couple of examples of the recent bid sections that you wrote. How did you go about it?

- What's your opinion of Bid winning probability assessment? What are the components that you would include in this assessment? In your experience, what % usually has resulted in higher success?

- Attention to detail is one of the biggest attributes of a bid manager. What processes and methods do you follow that nothing gets missed out in the end?

- What is the most outrageous feedback you received as part of a losing bid debriefing session?

- What is your management style?

- Describe the stress levels in your role and what do you do to manage it.

- How do you assess your proposal writer's skills and abilities?

- Have you been part of must-win deal proposal management? How did you approach it compared to a normal project bid?

- What is the split in terms of Government and Private sector bids that you have participated in the last year?

- Which vertical do you find it the most challenging to comply and respond? Give us a few examples.

- How many bids did you submit last year? Can you provide an approximate breakdown in terms of small, medium and large size bids?

- We all have had oversight in bids through our career. Can you provide couple of examples? How did it help you to manage it better for the future?

- Have there been instances where your submitted bid was disqualified due to compliance issues? What was the issue and how did it happen?

- What were the smallest and largest bids you ever submitted in terms of dollar value? What was their end result?

- The bid teams are under tremendous pressure to obtain the maximum technical points for each proposal section and there is a temptation to stretch the truth. Give couple of examples when your ethics was tested on the job.

Situational discussion points

- You have just been hired for this role and then you realize the firm is losing a lot of bids, embarrassments in front of clients (spelling mistakes, copying errors in the previous proposals etc.). What actionable steps would you undertake to position the firm for the future?

- You are participating in a client bid debriefing session. The feedback seems to be very unfair and process rigged to ensure the other vendor won. How do you ensure that you get the maximum benefit of this session?

- You have been asked to do bid support for a project. The proposal is almost ready. From some trusted sources or due to more exhaustive research, you find out the client's budget to an actual figure but do notice that your proposal pricing is above the client's budget. How do you handle this scenario?

Additionally, you can consider giving an old executive summary and ask the Bid Manager to provide their comments in terms of various parameters like writing quality, flow, narrative, persuasiveness etc.

Alternatively, consider giving a business problem statement and ask them to develop a 1 page executive summary.

12.20 Proposal writing books

There is an enormous amount of information available in terms of new ways of presentation, writing tips and tricks for an individual to upgrade one's knowledge and skills.

I have read the following three books

- "RFPs suck" by Tom Searcy,
- "Winner takes it all" by Scott Keyser
- "Proposal Best Practices: A Practical Guide to Improve Your Win Rate When Responding to RFPs by David Seibert

Some other notable books that you could potentially explore are:

- The Ultimate Bid and Proposal Compendium: The reference guide to winning bids, tenders and proposals by Christopher S Kalin

- Solution Engineering: Winning Proposals are Engineered, Not Just Written by Peter Lierni

- Powerful Proposals: How to Give Your Business the Winning Edge by Terry Bacon, David Pugh

- Federal Government Proposal Writing: Learn federal proposal writing from ground zero by George Brown

- Winning Government Business: Gaining the Competitive Advantage with Effective Proposals by Steve R. Osborne

- Getting in the Winner's Circle by Dick Close

- Shipley Proposal Guide by Larry Newman

- Shipley Capture Guide by Larry Newman

- Shipley Business Development Lifecycle Guide - Larry Newman
- The RFP Success Book by Lisa Rehurek
- Proposal Development Secrets by Matt Handal
- The Consultant's Guide to Results-Driven Business Proposals by Jack Philips
- Win More Business, Write Better Proposals by Michel Theriault
- Campaign to Win the 13 Commandments by Jay Heather
- The Capture Management Life-cycle - Winning more business by Gregory A. Garrett & Reginald J. Kipke

www.ingramcontent.com/pod-product-compliance
Lightning Source LLC
Chambersburg PA
CBHW060414220526
45465CB00008B/2885